ORTHO'S All About
Pruning

Written by Judy Lowe

Meredith® Books
Des Moines, Iowa

Ortho® Books
An imprint of Meredith® Books

All About Pruning
Editor: Marilyn Rogers
Contributing Editor: Leona H. Openshaw
Contributing Technical Editors: Bonnie Lee Appleton,
    E. Thomas Smiley
Art Director: Tom Wegner
Copy Chief: Catherine Hamrick
Copy and Production Editor: Terri Fredrickson
Contributing Copy Editors: Cynthia S. Howell,
    Carol Boker, Ed Malles
Technical Proofreader: John C. Fech
Contributing Proofreaders: Kathy Roth Eastman,
    Margaret Smith, Gretchen Kaufmann
Contributing Prop/Photo Stylists: Mary Klingaman,
    Diane Munkel
Indexer: Don Glassman
Electronic Production Coordinator: Paula Forest
Editorial and Design Assistants: Kathleen Stevens,
    Karen Schirm
Production Director: Douglas M. Johnston
Production Manager: Pam Kvitne
Assistant Prepress Manager: Marjorie J. Schenkelberg

Additional Editorial Contributions from
  Art Rep Services
Director: Chip Nadeau
Designers: Laura Rades, Shawn Wallace
Illustrator: Dave Brandon

Meredith® Books
Editor in Chief: James D. Blume
Design Director: Matt Strelecki
Managing Editor: Gregory H. Kayko
Executive Ortho Editor: Benjamin W. Allen

Director, Sales & Marketing, Retail: Michael A. Peterson
Director, Sales & Marketing, Special Markets:
    Rita McMullen
Director, Sales & Marketing, Home & Garden Center
    Channel: Ray Wolf
Director, Operations: George A. Susral

Vice President, General Manager: Jamie L. Martin

Meredith Publishing Group
President, Publishing Group: Christopher M. Little
Vice President, Consumer Marketing & Development:
    Hal Oringer

Meredith Corporation
Chairman and Chief Executive Officer: William T. Kerr
Chairman of the Executive Committee: E.T. Meredith III

Cover photograph: Bryan McCay

All of us at Ortho® Books are dedicated to providing you
with the information and ideas you need to enhance your
home and garden. We welcome your comments and
suggestions about this book. Write to us at:
    Meredith Corporation
    Ortho Books
    1716 Locust St.
    Des Moines, IA 50309–3023

Thanks to
Janet Anderson, Melissa George, Gina Hale, Ann Hiemstra,
Angie Hoogensen, Aimee Reiman, Mary Irene Swartz;
Heard Gardens, Johnston, Iowa

Photographers
(Photographers credited may retain copyright ©
    to the listed photographs.)
L= Left, R= Right, C= Center, B= Bottom, T= Top
William D. Adams: p. 22;
R. Todd Davis: p. 47 (B), 53 (L);
Alan & Linda Detrick: p. 3 (T), 4, 50, 82 (L);
Derek Fell: p. 23 (T);
Harrison L. Flint: p. 31 (B);
David Goldberg: p. 6 (B);
John Glover: p. 3 (B), 6 (T), 27, 30, 46 (B), 59 (R), 60 (T),
    75, 76, 84 (L);
Jerry Harpur: p. 24 (L);
Lynne Harrison: p. 57 (L);
Horticultural Photography: p. 40;
Jerry Howard/Positive Images: p. 16, 61;
Jeff Iles: p. 12 (B)
Andrew Lawson: p. 33, 44 (T), 47 (T), 59 (L), 68, 70,
    71 (R), 80 (R);
Stuart McCall: p. 28 (R);
Brian McCay: p. 11, 36;
David McDonald Photo Garden: p. 12 (TL), 26 (L), 42,
    79 (R);
Clive Nichols: p. 53 (R), 54 (T), 55 (B), 79 (L);
Jerry Pavia: p. 56 (BR);
Susan A. Roth: p. 3 (BC), 5 (C & B), 12 (TR), 25 (L),
    28 (L), 29, 32, 34, 43, 44 (B), 45 (L), 48, 49 (T), 51, 52,
    62 (B), 64, 72 (L), 73, 82 (R), 84 (R);
Richard Shiell: p. 24 (R), 31 (T), 37 (LB), 46 (T), 55 (T),
    56 (BL), 57 (R), 58, 60 (B), 66, 69 (T), 72 (R), 74, 77,
    85 (B);
Pam Spaulding/Positive Images: p. 3 (TC), 18;
The Studio Central: p. 14, 15;
Michael S. Thompson: p. 9, 13, 23 (B), 25 (R), 26 (R),
    45 (R), 69 (B), 71 (L), 78, 80 (L), 83, 87;
Kay Wheeler: p. 54 (B).

THE ART AND SCIENCE OF PRUNING

Guests feel welcome in this attractive entry garden. Proper pruning in the correct season prepares the dogwood, azalea, and spirea for abundant flowers and healthy foliage.

At first, pruning may seem a bit intimidating. But it really isn't. Like many other gardening techniques, pruning combines art and science. The science involves learning the simple rules of how plants grow, why they might need pruning, the best time to do it, and the proper techniques for each type of plant. Think of these as the principles of pruning. Once you've learned them, you will know exactly what to do, how to do it, and when. That's what this book is all about—answering the questions you might have, giving you step-by-step directions, and making you feel confident when you pick up a pruning saw or loppers.

The artistic side of pruning is an outgrowth of the scientific side. If you follow specific pruning techniques, your plants are going to look better and produce more flowers and fruit. But the pruner has some leeway to express his or her artistic temperament and imagination. In common with all art, pruning first calls for envisioning what the final result will be—then shaping the plant to what was visualized, keeping in mind all the while your style of landscaping and the natural look of each plant.

The main thing is to prune with a purpose, to realize what you want to accomplish. To do that, you need to know why and how proper pruning will help your plants, rather than hurt them.

WHY PRUNE?

Many people think of pruning only in connection with a shrub or tree that has grown too big for the spot where it's planted. But there are equally important reasons to prune that have nothing to do with size. Proper pruning also improves the condition and the appearance of your plants in numerous ways.

Timely pruning repairs damage before further problems can occur. It also encourages greater quantity and quality of fruit and flowers. Pruning can shape a plant so that it's more attractive and better able to withstand heavy snow and storms. It stimulates new growth and directs that growth where you want it to go. You can even use pruning to create living works of art in your landscape— a whimsical topiary elephant, for instance, or candelabra espalier.

Bougainvillea blooms on the current season's growth. Pruning at the right time ensures plenty of colorful blossoms.

Rather than picking up your hand pruners only when a shrub has grown out of bounds, look at the numerous benefits that regular pruning provides all your plants.

TO INCREASE FLOWERS AND FRUIT

What's the purpose of growing roses, raspberries, apples, or camellias? To produce plenty of flowers or fruit. How do you do that? One way is by pruning correctly. For instance, roses are borne only on what's called new wood, the current season's growth. Cutting back the stems of a rosebush early each spring stimulates new growth and therefore new flowers. If you want larger flowers and don't mind if there are fewer of them, disbud the rose. To do that, remove all of the buds on a stem, except the terminal one. Then the plant's energy is directed to that one bud, which grows large.

In a similar technique to ensure a larger fruit crop on apple trees, pick off some of the apples on each branch while they are still small and the ones remaining will grow bigger than if all were left to ripen. Another way is to thin a fruit tree to remove unproductive branches and open the center of the tree to sunlight.

Of course, you need to be careful about timing because pruning in the wrong season can decrease flowers or fruit. Cut back a forsythia during winter and it won't bloom much in spring because pruning has removed most of the flower buds, which grow on old wood. For specific advice on when, how, and whether to prune specific plants, check the encyclopedia entries in each chapter for the fruits, flowering shrubs, and trees in your yard.

TO PROMOTE COLORFUL BARK AND STEMS

The most attractive quality of some trees is their bark. Removing lower limbs over a period of three to four years helps show off

Removing the lower limbs of this lacebark pine shows off one of the tree's most attractive features—the mottled bark.

the bark on trees such as river birch and paperbark maple. To expose the mottled trunk of a crape myrtle so that it looks as interesting in winter as it does in summer, transform the shrub into a tree through careful pruning.

If you're fortunate to have redosier dogwood or Japanese kerria in your yard, you'll want to encourage new colorful stems, which are knockouts during cold weather. Do this by cutting one-fourth of the oldest stems back to the ground each year (see page 11).

TO DIRECT PLANT GROWTH

A plant doesn't always grow in the direction the owner would like. Two tree limbs may grow so close that they rub against each other, causing a wound. Branches of foundation shrubs may lean into the walkway so anyone on the way to the door has to brush against them. When rose stems grow toward the center of the bush instead of to the outside, black spot and mildew are more likely to develop. But pruning can easily correct these conditions and direct new growth where you want it to go.

An empty wall in the sun provides a perfect spot to train a shrub with flexible branches, such as pyracantha, into an espalier.

WHY PRUNE?
continued

If left unpruned, some shrubs spread wildly and become sparse in their center. For santolina, a small aromatic evergreen, head back clumps in early spring and shear off blooms after they fade.

TO CONTROL SIZE

The most common reason people prune is to control overgrown plants. The problem may be a shrub that's blocking the front walk or a tree that's crowding the fence. Possibly it's a rampant vine that looked pretty when it was young and small, but now seems determined to take over your yard. Often we don't pay attention to a particular plant until it is obvious something must be done to restrict its size. One day you look out your picture window and instead of seeing snow-capped mountains in the distance, you notice that a too-tall holly obstructs your view.

In the middle of the summer, cutting the plant down to size will be hot, sweaty work, and you still may not be pleased with its final appearance. Is there a better way?

As you'll learn throughout this book, a little pruning each year often prevents a shrub, tree, or vine from becoming too big and needing more extensive pruning. This is especially important for hedges, foundation plantings, and shrubs growing in front of windows because they need to remain a certain size.

This gradual pruning is often called annual pruning, and it's good both for the plants and for those who care for them. Annual pruning is good for the owner because it's easier to spend a few minutes cutting off a limb here and snipping back a stem there than it is to devote hours to trying to shape a plant that has grown large enough to obstruct a view. Frequent minimal pruning is best for the plant because small, selective cuts gently guide it to grow in the form and to the size you want without having to resort to major "surgery."

This is especially true for evergreens. Many can't be cut back beyond where the needles grow because new growth won't sprout from the old, bare branches. If you don't control the size of those evergreens when they're young, controlling and reshaping them may be difficult or impossible later on.

Annual pruning keeps plants at their optimum size for a space—with a minimal expense of time and effort.

TO INCREASE VIGOR

Regular pruning keeps plants vigorous and healthy. It encourages the growth of new branches, which will produce more flowers and resist insects and diseases better than old branches. When a plant is thinned of excess growth, its interior is opened up to light and air, which helps it to grow better and resist foliar diseases related to poor air circulation, such as powdery mildew.

On the other hand, pruning too much creates the potential for stimulating sucker growth or inviting diseases, such as fireblight, or insect pests, such as aphids.

TO REPAIR AND PREVENT DAMAGE

Broken branches and stems on trees and shrubs provide an entryway for insects and pathogens. Proper removal of branches will promote quicker wound closure and protect the tree. It's important to promptly cut out dead, diseased, or dying branches as soon as you notice them.

After frost damage, check to see whether buds appear to be alive before pruning. If they are, they should appear fat. Or, gently scrape the stems with your fingernail to see whether the tissues under the twig's bark are green (alive) or brown (dead). Always cut back to a live, outward-facing bud.

When branches or limbs cross, they rub against each other, creating a wound where pathogens and insects may enter. To prevent this, prune off one of the branches.

Some trees, such as Siberian elms and silver maples, have weak wood that often breaks under the weight of snow or in high winds. The branches of these trees often join the main trunk at a narrow angle. Branches that grow from the tree at less than a 45-degree angle are likely to be weakly attached and may split off from the tree. To correct, selectively remove branches attached at narrow angles when the tree is young, leaving branches with strong, wide angles that can withstand storms. Or, instead of removing all tight crotches, reduce the length of some of the branches, remove some, and leave some to remove next year. Total removal of all tight crotches may be too much in one year. Limit removal to one-fourth of the crown per year.

TO PROTECT PLANTS AND YOUR INVESTMENT IN THEM

Mature trees in good shape and well-formed shrubbery are valuable assets. Studies have shown that a pleasingly landscaped property sells faster and for more money than those that aren't as well landscaped or maintained. Proper pruning helps to keep your plants healthy and handsome, safeguarding your investment in them.

On the other hand, neglected trees can quickly become a liability. They might fall on your car, your fence, or your neighbor's house. Learn to notice signs that your trees need attention and prune out dead or dangerous limbs before the tree becomes hazardous and an accident happens.

Wide-angled crotches are strong because wood fibers in the trunk and branch are continuous. With narrower angles, bark grows between the branch and trunk and makes the crotch weak.

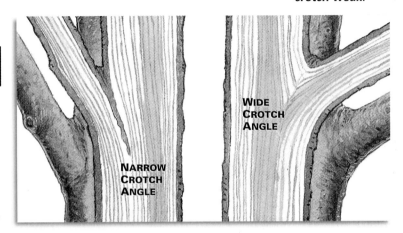

NARROW CROTCH ANGLE

WIDE CROTCH ANGLE

A goal for young trees is to remove weak branches, those joining the trunk at a 45-degree angle or less. Also, space branches at least 18 inches apart radially around the trunk but not above one another.

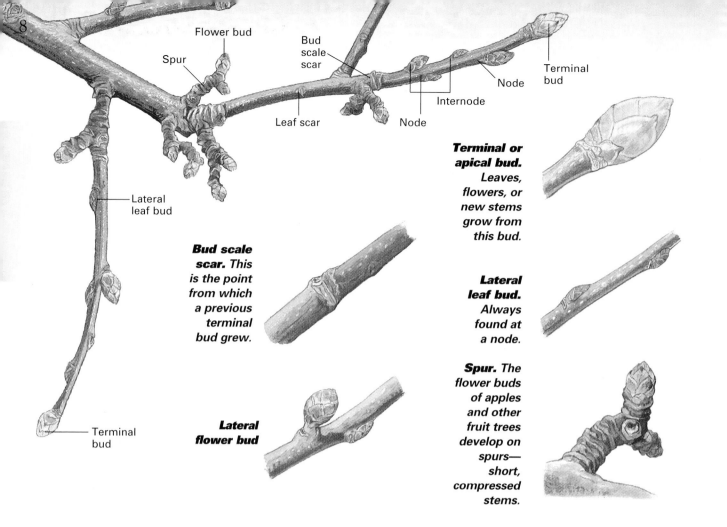

Flower bud

Spur

Bud scale scar

Node

Terminal bud

Internode

Node

Leaf scar

Lateral leaf bud

Terminal bud

Bud scale scar. *This is the point from which a previous terminal bud grew.*

Lateral flower bud

Terminal or apical bud. *Leaves, flowers, or new stems grow from this bud.*

Lateral leaf bud. *Always found at a node.*

Spur. *The flower buds of apples and other fruit trees develop on spurs— short, compressed stems.*

PRUNING AFFECTS GROWTH

When you understand how plants grow, it's easier to predict the response to pruning. This in turn makes it simpler to choose the right technique for each situation, whether you're pruning trees, shrubs, or vines.

PARTS OF A WOODY PLANT

One bare branch may look much like another to the untrained eye, but in reality, the branch tells the story of the tree with its buds, nodes, internodes, spurs, and scars.

BUDS are undeveloped, dormant shoots, usually protected by a covering of scales. Depending on the type of bud, they may produce leaves, stems, flowers, or fruit. The main difference between them is that flower buds are rounder and fatter than leaf buds.

NODES are the points at which buds develop and where leaves join the stem. Internodes are the portions of the stem between nodes.

SPURS are compressed stems on which flower buds and eventually fruit develop. Not all woody plants have them.

SCARS develop wherever a leaf or fruit falls from the stem. Terminal buds leave behind a scar that encircles the twig, called the bud scale scar. You can track the age of the stem by counting the bud scale scars.

TYPES OF BUDS

The bud on the tip of a branch is known as the terminal bud. It is the dominant and strongest-growing bud on the branch.

Pruning the terminal bud releases its hold over the other buds. The buds below the cut begin to grow, and two or more new stems develop.

Some plant species have alternate branching patterns (left). On others, leaves and stems grow opposite one another (right). Pruning an "opposite" plant usually results in two stems growing from one point.

Buds that grow along the sides of the stems at the nodes are called lateral buds. These are also called axillary buds because they are found in the axil between the leaf and the stem. They may generate flowers or leaves, and as the season progresses, they may grow into new stems.

Some species have accessory buds, flower buds that accompany lateral buds. Usually, they're found beside or above the lateral bud.

There are two other classifications of buds: dormant, also called latent, and adventitious. Dormant buds form over one growing season and produce leaves, stems, or flowers the next season. Adventitious buds can develop in places other than at the end of a twig or in leaf axils. They appear when pruning or wounding stimulates their development.

BRANCHING PATTERNS: A plant with two buds at a node, growing in opposite directions, has an opposite branching pattern. If only one bud grows from each node, and each bud develops on alternating sides of the stem, the arrangement of buds is called alternate and the plant has an alternate branching pattern. If there are three or more buds at one point on a stem, the branching pattern is called whorled.

REMOVING THE TERMINAL BUD

Terminal buds exercise what is called apical dominance on buds that grow farther back on the limb. They produce a hormone called auxin that inhibits growth of lateral buds. Apical dominance determines a plant's natural branching habit and its response to pruning. It produces orderly, controlled growth and gives plants their characteristic shape. A number of things happen to a plant after removing a terminal bud.

THE GROWTH PATTERN CHANGES. With the terminal bud gone, its apical dominance is eliminated. The growth pattern of the plant alters as dormant, latent or adventitious buds begin to grow. Lateral buds nearest the terminal bud are the first to expand, and side branches develop. Where one stem grew, two or more emerge. On alternate branching plants, only one new stem will develop from each node; opposite branching plants will develop two new stems at each node.

If you want to promote side branching, removing the terminal bud is the way to do it. However, anyone who simply wants a smaller plant won't be happy with the results and should choose another method.

ADVENTITIOUS BUDS DEVELOP.
If the branch is broken or cut far back into mature wood, adventitious buds will start to grow. These develop near the surface of a branch and not within deeper tissues, and so may form water sprouts—undesirable, weakly attached upright growths. Water sprouts easily break off in storms.

Water sprouts often burst from adventitious buds in bark after heavy pruning. Remove these as soon as they appear.

HOW TO PRUNE

Practically every homeowner has sheared a few inches from the stems of an overgrown shrub, hoping to make it smaller. Usually, the result is a shrub that is just as large, if not bigger and bushier, the next year. How you prune is as vitally important as when or why you prune.

To thin, cut stems off completely, clipping them back to a main branch.

PRUNING CUTS

A RULE OF THUMB FOR PRUNING

Beware of overpruning. While some plants tolerate heavy pruning, many do not. The general rule is to remove no more than one-fourth of a plant at one time and not more than one-third during one year. So, if a plant is overgrown or hasn't been trained properly, prune it over a period of four years rather than all at once. Otherwise, it may have a hard time recovering.

Each cut has its own specific results, and it's to your advantage to know them well. In fact, it would be almost impossible to realize your goals in pruning without knowing the effect of each type of cut.

THINNING: To thin a plant, you remove a lateral stem or limb back to a main branch, to the trunk, or to the ground. Thinning encourages the growth of the branches that remain while it maintains the natural habit of the plant. It also opens up the interior of the plant to more sunlight, which helps to keep the internal branches healthy.

You can keep a plant at the same height and width for many years through selective thinning. If an overgrown shrub is thinned instead of sheared, it won't regrow to be too large six months later. This is because the terminal buds are not removed and they continue to control growth.

HEADING: If you remove the terminal bud by cutting in no particular spot on the stem, you are using a heading cut. In this type of cut, apical dominance is lost and vigorous new growth develops from buds just below the cut. The result is new stems or branches clustered together, which can create such crowded conditions that the interior of the plant dies from lack of sunlight.

LATERAL PRUNING: A better type of heading cut is lateral pruning. This technique involves cutting a main stem back to a lateral bud or shoot that's pointing in the direction you would like the new growth to go (usually toward the outside of the plant). The lateral stem should be no smaller than a third to half the diameter of the cut stem. The unruly growth of heading cuts does not develop with lateral pruning because the lateral stem maintains apical dominance.

SHEARING: This involves shortening all stems by a certain amount, as in pruning a hedge with shears or an electric hedge trimmer. Robust new growth occurs just below

Thinning helps shrubs maintain their natural habit. It opens up the plant and stimulates the remaining stems into growth.

the cut. However, the stubs that result from this type of cut invite disease.

Shearing provides a formal appearance and needs to be repeated often and regularly to be effective. It is useful for hedges and topiary, but not for most shrubs or trees. The dense outer shell of leaves and stems blocks light to the inside of the plant, killing off leaves and stems in the interior. If the outer shell is injured, the damage may lead to more serious problems. Many plants do not sprout in this "dead zone," and an injury may prove fatal.

When heading, you remove the terminal bud by cutting anywhere on the main stem.

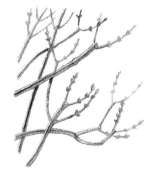

Lateral pruning, clipping the main stem back to a lateral bud or branch, encourages dense growth without twigginess.

PINCHING: No equipment is involved, making this the easiest method. With your thumb and forefinger, gently remove the tip of a plant's soft new growth. Gardeners often pinch the pine candles (young shoots before the needles expand) to ensure denser growth.

HOW MUCH TO PRUNE

Heavy pruning removes one-half or more of the growth. In the case of shrubs, it may refer to cutting the plant to the ground. Heavy pruning is used to renovate plants. Plants that grow vigorously can tolerate heavy pruning.

Light pruning involves removing one-fourth or less of the plant. This is used for low-growing plants and those that can't take heavy pruning.

CUTTING CORRECTLY

HOLDING PRUNERS: There's a right and a wrong way to hold pruning shears and loppers. Place the thin blade next to the trunk to avoid leaving stubs.

HOW TO CUT: For plants with alternate branches, make a slightly slanted cut about ¼ inch above a bud that's pointing in the direction you want new growth to go. The slant should angle away from the bud so rain doesn't stand at the base of the bud and rot it. With an opposite branching pattern, buds are in pairs, so make a flat cut that is equidistant from both. Or you can make a slanting cut to remove one of the two buds. When cutting back to main branches or to the trunk, prune just outside the collar (a raised or swollen area at the base of the branch, see page 23).

Shearing shortens stems to a similar height over all and encourages vigorous growth in a thin, outer layer of the plant.

For the cleanest, closest cut, hold pruning shears so the thin cutting blade is next to the main stem.

When pruning a small branch, cut on a slant away from the bud and about ¼ inch above it.

If cut too close, the bud may die; if cut too far, the stub provides an entrance for insects and diseases. At too sharp an angle, the bud ends up weakly attached to the stem. The correct cut is on the left.

WHEN TO PRUNE

When pruning azaleas, encourage a natural shape by trimming wayward growth and doing necessary thinning as soon as flowering has finished. Pruning later in the year, and shearing at the wrong time, as above, remove buds and, consequently, next year's crop of flowers.

In early spring, sap may flow from a pruning wound on some trees. It won't harm the tree but can be unsettling. Hold off on pruning until after weather warms to prevent "bleeding."

There isn't one time of year that's right for pruning every tree or shrub. Timing depends less on species than on your goal—whether you want flowers, fruit, or growth suppression. Plants as diverse as spring-flowering shrubs, roses, junipers, and deciduous trees are pruned during different seasons because timing affects their response.

WHAT TIME OF YEAR?

WINTER: Pruning deciduous plants in winter, when most plants are dormant (not growing), promotes fast regrowth in spring. It's also easier to prune at this time of year because with foliage out of the way, you can see the shape of the plant. Schedule pruning for the end of winter because wound closure begins in spring.

EARLY SPRING: Pruning just before new growth begins allows plants to recover quickly and stimulates growth.

SUMMER: Pruning in summer when plants are actively growing can damage a plant by exposing previously shaded tissue to full sun. The exposure may scorch the tissue. It may also dwarf a plant because it has to use energy to close the wounds left by pruning. This isn't all bad, however. With fast-growing hedges, summer pruning can subdue their growth. And hot-weather pruning minimizes the formation of suckers.

FALL: This is the worst time to shear plants because it encourages new growth that may not have time to harden off before winter. Consequently, the new growth may be killed by the cold. However, it's okay to thin plants in fall, especially after plants are dormant.

EXCEPTIONS TO THE RULES

Naturally, there are plants that don't fit the guidelines. Exceptions include needled evergreens, flowering trees and shrubs, and deciduous trees that "bleed" (ooze sap). Also, there are pruning chores you can do any time of the year: cutting off dead, diseased, or broken branches and removing suckers and water sprouts (vigorous shoots arising from stem tissue).

Most larger deciduous and evergreen trees can be safely pruned year-round as long as you avoid pruning elms during the flight times of elm bark beetles and avoid pruning oaks in April through June in areas where oak wilt is a problem.

In late spring or early summer, pinch the tips of stems to encourage bushiness. This includes candles of pines and other needled evergreens. However, don't remove flower buds of summer-flowering plants.

FLOWERING TREES AND SHRUBS

SPRING BLOOMERS: If you prune an evergreen azalea, forsythia, or other spring bloomers in late winter, it won't bloom that spring because you've removed the flower buds. Spring-flowering shrubs or trees should be pruned within a month after blooming. That's when plants begin forming the buds that will produce the next year's blossoms. Most spring bloomers flower on what's called year-old or previous season's growth.

SUMMER BLOOMERS: Shrubs and trees that flower in summer produce blooms on new growth and so are pruned in early spring. This encourages lots of vigorous growth and bud formation. Examples include butterfly bush, crape myrtle, and hibiscus.

Some plants produce blooms on both year-old branches and on new growth; others produce their flowers on branches that are two years old.

TREES THAT BLEED

Although many people are horrified to see a tree bleed sap, it only looks harmful. To avoid sap bleeding, don't prune birches, elms, maples, dogwoods, walnuts, and yellowwoods in late winter or in early spring when their sap is rising. Prune them in summer, after temperatures are warmer.

HOW OFTEN TO PRUNE

How frequently a plant requires pruning depends on its growth, shape, site, weather, and your reason for pruning. Plants in warm-winter climates and plants that grow quickly generally need more frequent pruning than slow-growing plants in cold regions. Some trees never need pruning except for occasional storm damage.

At the other extreme are formal hedges or shrubs that block a window. Once a month during the growing season, prune these plants to help keep them in bounds. (Or replace them with shrubs that fit the space.)

Most trees need more attention when they're young than they do after they've matured. Once you've trained them correctly, you will find that their maintenance time greatly diminishes.

Tall stewartia provides an attractive branching pattern even without foliage. In late winter, prune to maintain this look by thinning out crowded or dead branches. The tree's colorful bark also adds interest in every season.

PRUNING CALENDAR

EARLY SPRING
Prune summer-flowering trees and shrubs, which bloom on new growth, nonblooming broad-leaved evergreen plants, and evergreen or deciduous hedges. Also prune hybrid tea, floribunda, grandiflora, and miniature roses. Remove winter-killed growth from climbing and rambling roses.

LATE SPRING OR EARLY SUMMER
Prune spring-flowering shrubs immediately after their blossoms fade. Pinch or trim one-half of new candles on pines and other needled evergreens.

SUMMER
Shear deciduous or evergreen hedges. Prune mature climbing roses, which are more than two or three years old, and rambling roses after they bloom. Prune dogwoods, maples, walnuts, and yellowwoods, if needed. Prune summer-flowering shrubs and trees as blossoms fade.

FALL
Trim long rose canes. (If they remain, the winter wind will damage them and surrounding objects as wind whips them.)

WINTER
Prune berried shrubs or trees by harvesting for holiday decorations. Prune deciduous trees, fruit trees, and deciduous shrubs that don't flower in late winter or spring, but make sure the temperature is above 20° F.

TOOLS OF THE TRADE

Having the right tool for each job makes pruning easier and faster. Because high-quality tools can last a lifetime, take time to try them out before you buy. The tool should be balanced and feel comfortable in your hand. Today's tools are lighter and more comfortable than in the past. Look for ergonomic designs and lightweight materials that produce stronger action with less effort: slip-resistant handles, strong construction, contoured handles, cushioned grips, and gear or ratchet mechanisms. These can make pruning a pleasure even for those with little hand strength.

Taking care of your tools will keep them in good shape and make them last longer. Clean them after each use and rub them with a few drops of oil to prevent rust. Occasionally oil the moving parts so they'll operate smoothly. Always store them in a dry place.

Pole pruner

Bypass pruner

Ergonomic pruner with rotating handles

Anvil pruner

PRUNERS

A high-quality pair of hand pruners is the most important pruning tool because you will use them the most. They come in two main types: bypass and anvil. Use them to cut stems up to ¾ inch in diameter.

Straight anvil types have a sharp blade that cuts against a flat anvil. They rarely need adjusting and the blade is easily replaced, but often they crush a stem rather than cut it, especially if the blade is dull. For this reason, their use is often discouraged.

Bypass pruners have one sharp blade and one hooked anvil. They make clean cuts close to the stem, but can't be used on branches greater than ½ inch in diameter. A third type of pruner works like scissors, but is appropriate only for small twigs.

Pole pruners have either anvil or bypass pruners attached to a long wooden or fiberglass shaft. They're operated by a rope or handle on the pole. They are safer than standing on a ladder to cut high in a tree.

LOPPERS

For stems up to 1¾ inches in diameter, long-handled loppers (sometimes called lopping shears) are best. They give good leverage and allow you to reach into the base of an overgrown shrub. Loppers come in anvil and bypass styles. Ratcheted or geared models provide more power with less effort. When buying loppers, make sure that there is enough space between the handles so your fingers don't get pinched as handles close.

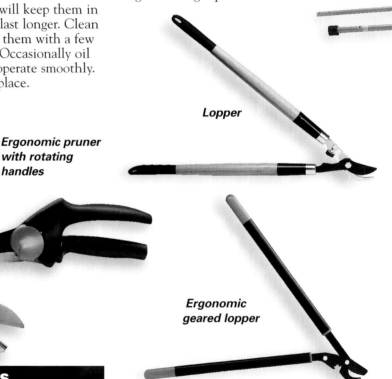

Lopper

Ergonomic geared lopper

SAWS

When a limb is too large for loppers, turn to a pruning saw, which can cut branches up to 4 or 5 inches in diameter. Large-toothed saws produce a rough edge. The smaller teeth of Japanese-type saws cut quickly and neatly. Carpenters saws aren't suitable for pruning because they're made to cut dry, not green, wood. Also, pruning saws cut on the pull stroke, as opposed to the push stroke on carpenters saws.

Folding saw

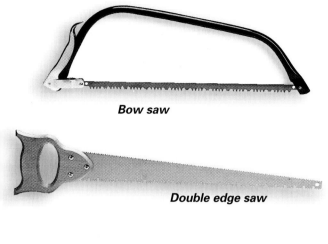

Bow saw

Double edge saw

Pole saw

Electric hedge shear

A folding saw is handy because it can be carried in a pocket. Use them for cutting smaller branches. Be certain the locking mechanism works well, or the saw can collapse while you're cutting. Most folding saws have curved blades, which are convenient when branches are crowded.

A bow saw is inexpensive, cuts quickly, and has a replaceable blade. Because of the bowed side, it can't always cut as close as other saws.

A saw with a wide blade is ideal for cutting larger limbs, but beware if it has two cutting edges. It's very easy to cut something you didn't mean to when there are sharp teeth on both sides of the saw.

For cutting overhead limbs up to 2 inches in diameter use a pole saw or extension saws.

Electric trimmers, which have a blade that oscillates, make fast work of shearing the top of a hedge evenly, but you have to be careful of the cord. Gas-powered models are also available, as are battery-powered shears. Always hold power shears with both hands.

CHAIN SAWS

A 12- to 16-inch chain saw is the most convenient size for homeowners. It can handle the largest pruning jobs that an amateur should tackle, while being lightweight and easy to maneuver. Chain saws can be dangerous. Observe safety rules by wearing safety glasses, a hard hat, and gloves, and keep both hands on the saw's handle at all times.

Chain saw

HEDGE SHEARS

Manual hedge shears are best for pruning hedges. Look for notched or wavy blades that do a good job of keeping the foliage from slipping out of your grasp. Lightweight handles and some kind of shock absorption are important if you do large quantities of hedge trimming.

SHARPENING YOUR PRUNING TOOLS

To sharpen pruners, loppers, or manual hedge shears, you'll need a whetstone or grindstone. Wet the stone with water or light oil and hold the blade against the stone. Move it against the sharp edge, as you would when sharpening a kitchen knife.

With bypass pruners, hone only the outside edge of the cutting blade. Sharpen both sides of the curved blade of anvil pruners so the blade will hit the flat edge evenly.

Leave saw-sharpening to a professional because it's a specialized technique. You can find a saw-sharpener by asking at a hardware store or lawn mower repair shop.

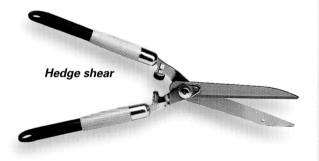

Hedge shear

SAFETY

For safety, hire an experienced, insured tree care professional when the pruning involves branches that are heavy, found high in the tree, or located near power lines.

Because pruning involves using sharp blades, power equipment, as well as puts you near limbs that can fall in unexpected directions and stems that can snap back, it's potentially one of the most hazardous gardening activities. Follow a few commonsense rules to avoid being harmed.

PROTECTIVE GEAR: Wear protective clothing and equipment every time you prune. This includes goggles, long pants and a long-sleeved shirt, thick gloves, and sturdy shoes with good traction. For overhead branches, add a hard hat. Use hearing protectors or earplugs with power equipment.

LADDERS: Never prune while standing on a ladder when working alone, nor use a chair instead of a ladder. Position the ladder's feet so that they don't wobble. The top of the ladder should rest firmly against a sturdy branch or crotch. Don't operate power equipment while on a ladder, nor stand on its top two steps. Take care when stepping off a ladder. Hire a professional to do any pruning that requires a ladder if you're not accustomed to working on one.

LOOK AROUND: Stay away from power lines. If there are wires in the tree, hire an arborist (tree care professional). If you are using a pole pruner or saw, stand to the side of where you expect branches to fall. Always be aware of the location of your power cords so you don't accidentally cut through them.

WEATHER: Quickly stop pruning and go indoors at the first sign of lightning. Even after the storm has passed, it's

Work smart: Don't stretch too far or stand beneath the branch (as at right). You will lose control of the pruner and may damage yourself as well as the tree. Never prune from a ladder (far right) while alone. And, don't stand on the top two rungs of the ladder.

Be smart: Don't prune near electrical lines. Call a tree care professional, who has the proper equipment and training, to do the job for you.

SAFETY CHECKLIST FOR PRUNING

■ Always use common sense when working with sharp pruning saws, electric shears, or chain saws.

■ Check for electrical lines and dead or hanging branches before beginning.

■ Consider where the branch will fall when it is cut or dropped from the tree. Make sure no one will be hit or that it will not knock over the ladder.

■ Use a stepladder or tie an extension ladder securely to the tree. Keep one hand on the ladder and one on the saw.

■ Station a helper on the ground as a lookout and safety checker.

■ Wear nonskid rubber-soled shoes, snugly fitting clothing, and leather gloves.

■ If you use a chain saw, wear leather boots.

■ It is advisable to wear a hard hat and protective glasses because you can easily bump into a branch and scratch an eye or lose a contact lens.

■ Call a professional if you lack proper equipment or if the branches to be removed are heavy or too high to reach safely.

still not safe to operate electric hedge trimmers or a chain saw. You can slip and fall or be electrocuted when the ground and plants are wet.

CHAIN SAW TIPS: Chain saws are the most hazardous tool used in pruning. To reduce the dangers, read the owner's manual and follow its instructions closely. Also, wear the recommended safety gear, especially eye and ear protection. Don't use a chain saw if you have to reach above your shoulders to cut, and never climb onto a ladder or into a tree with a chain saw. Always hold the saw firmly and correctly. Turn off the saw before walking anywhere with it. Be alert for kickback, where the guidebar of the chain saw suddenly kicks back toward the operator.

KNOW WHEN TO HIRE AN ARBORIST

Hire a professional when you feel the least bit uncomfortable about doing a pruning job yourself. Also let a pro evaluate your tree for insects and diseases, and do any cabling, bracing, work near power lines, pruning high in mature trees, and any job that requires tools you don't have.

Contact the International Society of Arboriculture, 217-355-9411 or write ISA at P.O. Box 3129, Champaign, IL 61826-3129 for a list of certified arborists in your area (on the Internet at www.ag.uiuc.edu/~isa). Its members have passed an examination and have at least three years experience.

The National Society of Arborists is a trade association of tree-care professionals. For a list of members, call 800-733-2622 or visit the website at www.natlarb.com.

Ask a tree service company to show proof of adequate liability insurance and workers' compensation for any accidents that might occur on your property. Also ask for and check out the company's local references. Try to talk to previous customers. Get an estimate and contract in writing and request that the bid include removal of all debris.

Don't hire someone who goes door to door looking for tree work, who climbs into live trees wearing spikes, or who offers to "top" your trees. These aren't accepted practices.

KEEP PLANTS SAFE, TOO

You can avoid ragged or torn bark by keeping your tools sharp and using the right-sized tool. A jagged cut will result when a 2-inch limb is cut with hand pruners. The same is true of cutting off a large branch in one step rather than in three.

PRUNING
DECIDUOUS TREES

Careful training of a young tree, such as this dogwood, to maintain its natural shape results in a mature specimen that requires little pruning.

The adage to "train up a child in the way he should go and when he is old, he will not depart from it," applies to young trees as readily as it does to children. A tree doesn't develop into a handsome mature specimen by accident. Its well-spaced branches and broad crown result from careful selection, correct planting, and regular, early pruning.

YOUNG TREES

A modest investment of time and effort over a tree's first four or five years will pay big dividends later on. Pruning to correct a large tree is expensive and creates slow-closing wounds. Most young trees, on the other hand, quickly recover from pruning. Some of the tasks for the early years:

■ Cut off broken branches so they won't become magnets for insects or pathogens.
■ Dig up suckers, vigorous upright growth from roots. Also, remove water sprouts, fast-growing shoots that are weakly attached to limbs.
■ For certain species, train the tree to a central leader, or one main stem. Remove competing leaders to give the tree a better form and make it more structurally sound.

■ Prune branches that join the trunk at a narrow angle, leaving branches with wide, and therefore strong, evenly spaced angles. (Exceptions are trees with upright forms.)
■ Remove any branch that crosses over or rubs against another.

In this chapter you'll learn how and why to train young trees. We'll follow the principles outlined in the previous chapter: Use thinning or lateral cuts, do the work at the recommended time of year for the particular tree, and practice safety.

TRAINING YOUNG TREES

When training a young tree, imagine what it will look like when it is older. As the illustrations show, trees have a variety of shapes. Part of your early pruning will be to develop the tree's shape and to help the tree grow up strong.

With a new tree, only prune limbs broken or damaged in transit. Make cuts close to the trunk but outside the collar. Nothing else is needed the first year except to prune diseased growth and damaged or dead branches. The time to actually begin guiding the young tree is during the second year after

TREE SHAPES

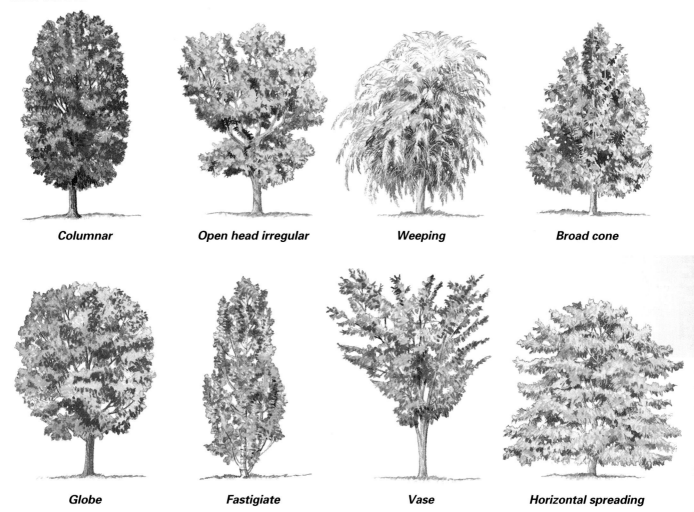

Columnar   Open head irregular   Weeping   Broad cone

Globe   Fastigiate   Vase   Horizontal spreading

planting. The most common goal is to develop a natural-looking tree. However, in confined spaces or in a formal garden there may be different goals.

For that reason, the first step in training trees is to select a goal: Do you want a natural-looking tree, one with a small size, or perhaps a formal shape? Each goal requires a different pruning strategy. Some trees won't need much training. Others, such as 'Bradford' pear, must be trained and pruned to avoid narrow crotches. If this isn't done, its limbs will eventually split away from the trunk, destroying the tree's shape.

DEVELOP A CENTRAL LEADER: Starting the second year after planting, develop a strong central leader in the tree. Central leader refers to the main trunk of the tree from which the branches grow. To develop a central leader, use thinning cuts, as illustrated in the previous chapter, to remove all but the strongest, most vigorous, or most central of the upright-growing branches. Training a tree to one central leader gives the tree the sturdiest branching structure possible, even in trees that develop multiple leaders with age.

SELECT SCAFFOLD BRANCHES: The second task is to develop the scaffolds. These are the large branches that are the framework of the tree. Begin this task in the tree's third or fourth year. It will take two to three years to complete the process.

The spacing of scaffolds is important. The rule of thumb for vertical spacing is 3 percent of the tree's mature height. Therefore, on a tree that will eventually grow 50 feet tall, keep the scaffolds about 18 inches apart. Choose limbs that are evenly distributed around the trunk and not too close to each other nor directly above one another. Also, the scaffolds should be at least 6 feet off the ground to allow traffic underneath the tree.

Another important quality is the angle at which the limb joins the trunk. Avoid angles narrower than 45 degrees (see the illustration on page 7). The wider the angle at which the trunk and branches join, the stronger their attachment. Ideally, the branches should approximate a clock, growing at 10 or 2 o'clock (with the trunk being 12).

A third quality to look for is the diameter of the limb. A scaffold that is smaller in

YOUNG TREES
continued

diameter than the trunk to which it is attached will be stronger and less likely to split from the trunk than one that's the same size as the trunk.

TEMPORARY BRANCHES: Don't overprune. It's true that in its early years, the tree may have limbs low on the trunk and more leaves and branches on its bottom than on the top. But those are actually good things for the tree. Leaving the lower limbs helps the trunk grow thicker and protects the bark from the sun. The foliage on the lower limbs means more growth for the tree. However, if a limb grows so far out as to make walking around the tree difficult, you can trim it back.

Be aware that most trees sold at nurseries have been extensively pruned, and these lower limbs may already have been removed.

To allow traffic under a tree, remove the lowest branches when they reach about an inch in diameter. Raise the crown of the tree by cutting off one-third of the lower branches each year for three years in late winter.

CORRECTING WEAK CROTCHES: When a limb and trunk join at a narrow angle, bark in the crotch dies and the branch weakens. Under stress, the limb is likely to break.

Prune narrow crotches when the tree is young. If you inherit a mature tree with weak narrow crotches, professional arborists can brace or cable the branches to prevent breaking. Generally, branches that are less than 4 to 6 inches in diameter are removed; larger limbs are braced or laterally pruned.

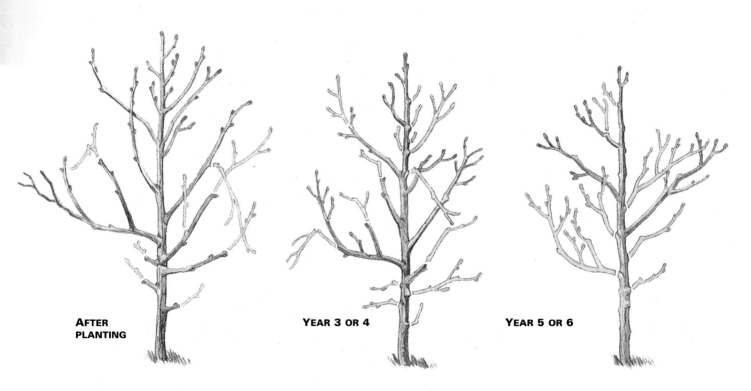

AFTER PLANTING

YEAR 3 OR 4

YEAR 5 OR 6

After planting: Prune only broken or damaged branches. Pruning more than that forces trees to expend energy replacing shoots rather than growing roots. Each year as you undertake training the tree, remind yourself that it's always better to underprune.

Year 3 or 4: Begin removing the branches on the lowest third of the trunk (if the nursery hadn't done this earlier). Select the scaffolds: three to four branches with wide angles radially spaced around the trunk 18 to 24 inches apart. Shorten unusually long branches in the center third of the tree.

Year 5 or 6: Prune all branches within 6 feet of the ground. Thin the crown to let in light and air. Once the well-trained tree reaches maturity, little other pruning is needed.

MATURE TREES

While a deciduous tree that was properly trained when young needs much less pruning than one that wasn't, a mature specimen may still require some attention. Limbs can sustain damage from insects, disease, and accidents. Branches may cross or rub against one another, or the tree may grow into power lines. However, if the tree was neglected when young, or if it has outgrown its location, it may require more extensive pruning.

If the tree is old or declining, it is preferable to perform what is called crown cleaning (removing the dead, dying, diseased, crossing, and structurally unsound branches). This is best done on a regular cycle of about one to three years. Most mature trees need only the regular crown cleaning, although some may require crown raising, crown thinning, or crown reduction (see page 22).

CROSSING OR RUBBING BRANCHES: During the winter, after the leaves have fallen, crossed or rubbing branches are most easily observed. Branches that are too close together destroy the scaffold branching pattern you've established, and they compete with one another for nutrients, water, and sunlight. When they rub together, they create a wound that can open the way for insects and disease to attack the tree.

Some species of trees produce more crossing branches than others. For example, owners of mature redbuds will have to pay attention to crossing branches, but those who planted red oaks will generally not have to deal with them.

WATER SPROUTS AND SUCKERS: Water sprouts are soft, flexible shoots that rapidly grow upward from main branches. They often appear from latent or adventitious buds after excessive or improper pruning.

Water sprouts drain energy from the tree. They are weakly attached to the tree, and they can become the target of insects. Get rid of them as soon as they appear.

Suckers are growths similar to water sprouts that appear on or at the base of the tree. They grow from the tree's roots. To control suckers, prune them.

Like water sprouts, suckers should be removed immediately. Besides being unsightly, they are weakly attached to the tree and can be the target of insects and diseases.

MAINTAINING THE CENTRAL LEADER: If a mature tree develops a competing leader, resist the urge to immediately cut it off. Instead, reduce the secondary leader by one-third each year for three years. Some trees, such as maples, oaks, and lindens, often develop competing leaders. Remove one-third of these as well (in trees up to 15 years old), to preserve the tree's structure.

Subduing competing leaders over a few years slows down their growth and encourages the tree to develop a stronger main leader with wide-angled scaffold branches. As the tree matures, multiple leaders may form; however, they will be less dominant than the principal leader and the tree's structure will be better able to withstand high winds and storms.

If, for some reason, your only choice is to cut back the central leader, prune it to a strong lateral upright branch that has about the same diameter or is no more than one-

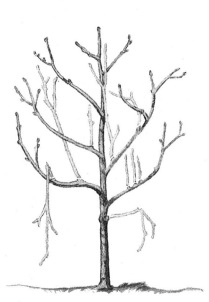

Both crossed branches and water sprouts have developed on the mature tree at left. Remove crossed or rubbing branches because they compete with one another for nutrients and create wounds that invite insects and diseases. Water sprouts, growing upward from main branches, drain energy from the tree. Remove them as soon as they appear. Also, remove dead and damaged wood as soon as it appears.

MATURE TREES
continued

third smaller. With time, this branch will assume apical dominance.

If a tree is growing into power lines or against your house, it may become necessary to reduce its height or its spread by lateral pruning. For mature trees this is best left to professional tree trimmers.

CROWN THINNING AND REDUCTION:
Thinning the crown, or upper portion of the branches, is the process of removing some limbs for the good of the tree. Thinning lets more light and air into the tree, which discourages fungal diseases and promotes good health. When fast-growing trees are thinned, their resistance to wind is reduced, and they aren't as likely to lose limbs in storms.

If a rapidly growing tree is producing lots of spindly new growth, the top may become larger than the roots can support. When the crown of such a tree is thinned, the demand on the roots is lessened and, therefore, balance is restored.

However, thinning is one of the most misused arboricultural practices. Few mature trees need it. If overdone, it leads to the "10-year takedown syndrome"—thin the tree

Developing a strong central leader (or main trunk) is important to many trees. If one or more competing leaders develop, remove them in stages—a third at a time over three years.

DON'T TOP TREES

Neither crown thinning nor reduction destroys the natural shape of the tree; topping does. Instead of using thinning cuts back to a main branch or to the tree's trunk, topping involves heading branches back to random stubs or small lateral branches.

The problems this causes are numerous: decaying stubs, sunburn from lack of leaves, water sprouts instead of healthy new growth, and stress from the loss of foliage and tissue. As explained in "Pruning Techniques," heading or topping activates numerous latent buds, which results in multiple weak shoots growing below each cut. And, because the shoots grow quickly, the tree will soon need pruning again. If a tree has been topped, it can be improved by

removing some of the water sprouts.

An alternative to topping is pollarding. Here, the shoots are cut to the main branch every year. Common in Europe, pollarding creates a thick tuft of small branches and keeps the tree at the same height.

now and in 10 years you'll have to remove it because pruning off too much leaf area from a mature tree will kill it—slowly.

Thinning is typically done only on rapidly growing trees of intermediate size. Mature trees should be thinned only if they are overly dense or likely to fail if not thinned.

To thin a tree, first, clean the crown—remove any dead, dying, or crossing limbs. Then remove live branches evenly along the limb. Because there usually are more branches near the ends of limbs, take more off the ends than from the center. Removing only interior limbs (sometimes called "lion's tailing") is a damaging and improper practice.

Before thinning a tree's crown, reread pages 10 and 11, which explain and illustrate this pruning technique, and pages 18 and 19, which show the natural shapes of trees. Also, Check out the top photo at right to ensure you recognize the collar on a tree branch.

CROWN RAISING: If the lower branches of a mature tree create a hazard or obstruct traffic—perhaps getting broken by the tops of passing semis—you can raise the tree's crown to eliminate the problem. Another common reason to raise the crown is to allow more sunlight directly under a shade tree for growing lawn or flowers.

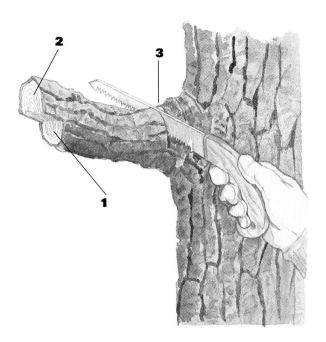

Remove a large, heavy branch in three cuts: First cut under the branch one-third of the way through. Then cut from the top of the branch 1 to 3 inches farther from the trunk until the branch falls. Remove the remaining stub.

Raise the crown of a mature tree just as you would a younger one—gradually, over a number of years. Be sure to cut carefully, so as not to introduce disease, and to incorporate these cuts into your normal maintenance. That is, as you inspect your tree for weak branches, take off those that fit into your crown raising plan first.

If for some reason you need to speed up this process, thinning back to upright-growing laterals can be done.

MAKING THE CUT: A tree's response to pruning depends greatly on where and how the cut is made. Tree pruning cuts should almost always be thinning cuts, which remove the branch back to where it is attached to the parent limb or to the trunk. Cuts that remove only portions of branches may result in decay and growth of excessive sprouts.

Make all cuts just outside the swollen branch collar (see photos at right), not flush with the trunk. The collar stores a compound that is toxic to decay-causing organisms. Removing or cutting into the collar causes the tree to lose this protective barrier. It also causes the wound to close slower.

When it becomes necessary to remove a large, heavy limb, use three cuts. Don't try to do it with one cut, which can rip the bark from the tree. For the first cut, make an undercut one-third of the way through the branch at a point between 6 and 12 inches from the trunk. Make the second cut from the

top of the branch about 1 to 3 inches farther from the trunk than the first cut, removing the branch. With the last cut, remove the short stub that's left, cutting at the outer edge of the branch collar. If working in a tight area, you may need to make the cut from the bottom to achieve the correct angle.

CLOSING WOUNDS: To encourage wounds made by tree pruning to close quickly, cut cleanly and smoothly with sharp saws or loppers, taking care to leave no ragged edges.

A cut on a tree doesn't heal the way a cut on your finger does. A tree closes the wound and isolates or compartmentalizes the injured area to form a barrier to decay. Callus tissue (an unorganized mass of cells) forms around the wound, appearing first as a circle and later as more doughnut shaped. Over time, the wound completely closes. If the cut develops more callus on the sides than on the top or bottom, it was probably made too close to the trunk.

WOUND DRESSINGS: Research has shown that wound dressings rarely help and can, in fact, harm a tree. Experts almost never recommend applying them. Exceptions to this involve oaks in areas where oak wilt is a problem and, for aesthetic reasons, when large cuts have been made. Some wound treatments may help suppress suckers and water sprouts. Maintain-A® and Tre-Hold® reduce sprout growth by about 50 percent.

CORRECTING BAD PRUNING: Although it may take a number of years, some trees that were pruned incorrectly can be improved. When trees are headed, they often have quite a few vertical branches. First, reduce the number of verticals to just a few on each main limb, then thin these back to a lateral branch. This process will open the interior of the tree to more light and air. At first, these branches will be only weakly attached, but over time they will strengthen.

If you encounter crossed branches, remove them, even if this leads to a gap in the canopy. The opening will eventually fill in. When you start to correct a poorly pruned tree, keep on the lookout for hidden decay in the branch stubs. If you find decay, prune the branches back to healthy wood.

The collar is a swollen lump at the base of a branch. Avoid cutting it when pruning. It contains substances that prevent insects and diseases from attacking the wound.

When a limb is properly pruned, callus tissue will gradually grow over the wound from the outer edges. Leaving the collar ensures fast closure.

ENCYCLOPEDIA OF DECIDUOUS TREES

ACER

Maples

GOAL: For large, strong maples such as Norway (A. *platanoides*), red (A. *rubrum*), and sugar (A. *saccharum*) maple, preserve the central leader and keep scaffolds widely spaced. For small, multi-trunked maples such as Japanese maple (A. *palmatum*), maintain the tree's natural shape. With brittle, weak-wooded maples such as silver (A. *saccharinum*) maple, prune to produce strong branches that resist storm damage.

HOW TO PRUNE: Most maples need little pruning beyond removing crossing limbs and dead branches and maintaining a central

Sugar maple

leader. To strengthen weak-wooded maples, prune away narrow crotches and train for wide-angled scaffold branches. Thin crowns of box elder (A. *negundo*), silver, and Norway maples to decrease wind resistance, if necessary. Maintain airy layered look of Japanese maple through thinning cuts.

WHEN: Summer, fall, early winter.

TIP: Maples will bleed when pruned in late spring; this doesn't harm them.

AESCULUS

Horsechestnuts, buckeyes

GOAL: Maintain natural shape and prevent branches from becoming crowded.

HOW TO PRUNE: Needs little pruning. Cut out dead and crossing branches and those that form narrow crotch angles. Thin crown of mature tree if it becomes too dense.

WHEN: Late spring, after bloom; summer; fall; winter.

TIP: Trees are pyramidal when young but develop rounded crowns when mature.

AILANTHUS ALTISSIMA

Tree of heaven

GOAL: Develop a strong structural framework. Decrease weight on long horizontal stems and develop strong crotches.

HOW TO PRUNE: Remove narrow crotches and suckers while young. Thin side branches from horizontal stems or laterally prune them. Repair damage.

WHEN: Winter.

TIP: Fast grower and weak wooded. Remove dead, damaged, and diseased limbs as often as necessary.

ALBIZIA JULIBRISSIN

Mimosa

GOAL: Maintain graceful spreading shape and minimize weak limbs.

HOW TO PRUNE: Over three years, raise the crown, removing lower limbs. When the tree reaches desired height, reduce the central leader to maintain size and encourage umbrella shape. Thin branches to decrease weight and reduce breakage.

WHEN: Mild climates: winter. Cold-winter areas: after the chance of frost has passed.

TIP: Rapid grower, but short-lived.

Mimosa

ALNUS

Alders

GOAL: Develop a strong structural framework.
HOW TO PRUNE: Train to a single- or multi-trunked tree and remove lower limbs. Remove dead branches. Needs little other pruning.
WHEN: Winter.

Serviceberry

AMELANCHIER CANADENSIS

Serviceberry, shadbush, and juneberry

GOAL: Preserve natural form.
HOW TO PRUNE: Use thinning cuts to maintain shape. Needs minimal pruning.
WHEN: Late spring, after flowering.
TIP: Can train to a single trunk or allow the tree to develop multiple trunks.

BETULA

Birches

GOAL: Over several years, limb up to expose attractive bark on the trunk.
HOW TO PRUNE: Remove dead branches, weak crotches, and diseased wood. European and canoe birches do not respond well to pruning because they heal slowly.
WHEN: Summer.
TIP: Pruning in late winter will cause bleeding, which stains the trunk.

CARPINUS

Hornbeams

GOAL: Maintain naturally graceful, pyramidal shape.
HOW TO PRUNE: Little pruning necessary. Use thinning cuts to maintain shape.
WHEN: Late winter/early spring.
TIP: Slow grower.

CARYA ILLINOINENSIS

Pecan

GOAL: Develop a strong framework.
HOW TO PRUNE: To develop central leader and scaffold branches that join the trunk at wide angles, cut back to 4 feet tall at planting time. In summer, choose the most vigorous sprout to become the leader and stake it. The following winter, prune the leader to just above a strong bud to stimulate growth of lateral branches. Beginning the next winter, choose scaffolds that are widely spaced and at least 6 feet above the ground. Remove branches that don't have wide angles. Other pruning is not needed except for removing dead or damaged branches.
WHEN: Late winter to early spring.

CATALPA

Catalpas

GOAL: Develop a strong structural framework and remove dead, damaged, and diseased limbs as often as necessary.
HOW TO PRUNE: Over a period of three or four years, remove lower limbs to develop a crown 8 to 12 feet above the ground. Because limbs tend to be weak, may need to laterally prune heavy branches to decrease weight.
WHEN: Winter.
TIP: Europeans often pollard common catalpa (*C. bignonioides*).

CELTIS

Hackberry, sugarberry

GOAL: Develop a strong structural framework; create a tall, clean trunk; and remove pendulous branches and weak crotches.
HOW TO PRUNE: When hackberry is young but older than three years, remove branches below 8 feet. Correct narrow crotches with thinning cuts.
WHEN: Winter.

Paper birch

ENCYCLOPEDIA OF DECIDUOUS TREES
continued

Katsura

CERCIDIPHYLLUM JAPONICUM

Katsura tree

GOAL: Develop a strong structural framework and maintain conical crown and upright branching.
HOW TO PRUNE: To train as a single-trunked tree, thin out competing leaders and branches. Mature single-trunk trees require minimal pruning. Thin horizontal spreading branches on multi-trunked trees to reduce weight and breakage.
WHEN: Early spring.
TIP: Doesn't tolerate hard pruning.

CERCIS CANADENSIS

Redbud

GOAL: Develop a strong structural framework, remove dead wood and weak growth, and maintain a spreading canopy.
HOW TO PRUNE: Remove dead and crossing branches. Use thinning cuts to maintain natural zigzag branching pattern and plant habit. Minimize pruning to avoid wounds and risk of disease.
WHEN: Winter or after flowering.
TIP: Flowers appear on older wood, including large branches and the tree trunk.

CHIONANTHUS VIRGINICUS

Fringe tree

GOAL: Develop the picturesque, open, spreading shape characteristic of fringe trees.
HOW TO PRUNE: Needs little pruning.
WHEN: Spring, after flowering.
TIP: Sometimes grown as a large shrub.

CLADRASTIS LUTEA

Yellowwood

GOAL: Develop a strong structural framework.
HOW TO PRUNE: Train to a central leader and remove narrow crotch angles. Prevent competition with the leader by shortening side branches to an outside lateral branch or bud.
WHEN: Winter.
TIP: Grows upright when young but spreads to a vase shape when mature. Has brittle branches.

CORNUS

Dogwoods

GOAL: For flowering (*C. florida*) and giant (*C. controversa*) dogwoods, maintain the horizontally layered branching pattern. For kousa dogwood (*C. kousa*), maintain the vase shape.
HOW TO PRUNE: Remove crossing branches and water sprouts. Leave lowest

Variegated giant dogwood

limbs at 2 to 3 feet above ground level. Use thinning cuts to maintain horizontal branching. In cold regions, leave the lowest branches on the trunk to protect it from cold.
WHEN: After flowering.
TIP: Spring pruning causes bleeding.

CRATAEGUS

Hawthorns

GOAL: Maintain broad-spreading to rounded form with branches beginning 6 feet up.
HOW TO PRUNE: Train to a central leader. Remove crossing branches and suckers. Over a period of three to four years, remove lower limbs to avoid contact with thorns.
WHEN: Late winter.
TIP: If fireblight strikes your tree, cut off the diseased area along with 6 to 12 inches of healthy tissue. Disinfect pruning tools between each cut. English hawthorn (*C. laevigata*) may be sheared as a hedge.

DAVIDIA INVOLUCRATA

Dove tree, handkerchief tree

GOAL: Maintain the distinctive broadly pyramidal growth habit and keep limbs high enough that people can walk beneath the tree and look up to see the white flowers.
HOW TO PRUNE: Train to a central leader. Remove dead and crossing branches.
WHEN: Prune immediately after flowering.
TIP: Large cuts close poorly.

DELONIX REGIA

Royal poinciana

GOAL: Develop a strong structural framework and maintain the spreading crown.
HOW TO PRUNE: To create a scaffold of five evenly-spaced branches starting 6 feet high above the ground, train to a central leader with scaffolding branches evenly spaced around trunk. Mature trees require little pruning.
WHEN: Late winter.

ELAEAGNUS ANGUSTIFOLIA

Russian olive

GOAL: Develop a strong structural framework and remove dead, damaged, and diseased limbs as often as necessary.
HOW TO PRUNE: Prune to central leader. To encourage strong central leader and wide-angled scaffolding branches when young and to develop strong branches, remove branches that join the trunk at a narrow angle. Laterally prune branches of mature trees so they don't become overly long and snap in storms.
WHEN: Winter or midsummer.
TIP: Responds to hard pruning and shearing.

FAGUS

Beeches

Common beech

GOAL: Develop a strong structural framework and maintain a central leader because multiple leaders can split as they age.
HOW TO PRUNE: Train to a central leader and encourage wide crotch angles. Tree may branch all the way to the ground. If you don't like this effect, remove lower limbs gradually over four years, after the tree is six to eight years old. Before then, the limbs protect the trunk from sunscald and help strengthen the leader.
WHEN: Winter.
TIP: Limbs can suddenly fall off mature trees. Does not tolerate heavy pruning.

FRANKLINIA ALATAMAHA

Franklinia, franklin tree

GOAL: Develop a strong structural framework and maintain upright crown.
HOW TO PRUNE: Requires little pruning except removal of dead branches and suckers.
WHEN: Winter, before flowering.

FRAXINUS

Ashes

GOAL: Develop a strong central leader
HOW TO PRUNE: Train when young to develop best form. To encourage natural shape, train the tree to a central leader with wide-angled scaffolds. Remove lower limbs over three or four years.
WHEN: Winter when dormant.
TIP: Green ash has an irregular crown and a spreading habit when mature, but some hybrids are pyramidal in shape.

Ginkgo

GINKGO BILOBA

Ginkgo

GOAL: Develop a strong strong central leader and prevent development of multiple trunks, which weaken mature specimens.
HOW TO PRUNE: Not much needed except training to a central leader and removal of lower limbs as needed over three or four years. Remove dead or diseased wood and suckers that develop.
WHEN: Early spring.
TIP: Trees change as they age. Young trees are sparsely branched and pyramidal in outline; mature trees are more densely branched and broad spreading.

ENCYCLOPEDIA OF DECIDUOUS TREES
continued

GLEDITSIA TRIACANTHOS INERMIS

Thornless honeylocust

GOAL: In young trees, control vigorous, extra-long growth; develop good structure.
HOW TO PRUNE: In early years, train so the tree has well-spaced lateral branches emerging from a single trunk. Head back unruly new growth, which may appear.
WHEN: Winter.
TIP: Withstands heavy pruning, but rarely needs it unless older tree loses vigor. Mature tree develops an opened-crowned vase shape.

GYMNOCLADUS DIOICA

Kentucky coffeetree

GOAL: Encourage narrow, round-headed form with strong branches.
HOW TO PRUNE: Train to a central leader with three to four scaffold stems. Little other pruning is necessary except removal of dead or diseased branches.
WHEN: Winter.

HALESIA CAROLINA

Carolina silverbell

GOAL: Develop a strong framework; maintain narrow canopy with ascending stems.
HOW TO PRUNE: Train to a central leader when young, with branches that begin about 3 to 4 feet above the ground. If a mature tree isn't blooming well, remove up to one-fourth of the oldest branches to stimulate new growth and bloom the next year. Established trees require only regular grooming.
WHEN: After flowering.
TIP: Although often grown as a multi-stemmed shrub, it looks best when trained to a central trunk. Silverbell habit may be irregular, which adds to the tree's charm.

Carolina silverbell

JACARANDA ACUTIFOLIA

Jacaranda

GOAL: Develop a strong structural framework and maintain natural open, irregular form.
HOW TO PRUNE: Train to a single leader or multiple trunks, as preferred. Remove winter damage. Remove vigorous vertical-growing side branches, which form narrow crotch angles. Occasionally thin mature trees.
WHEN: Early spring.

JUGLANS

Walnuts

GOAL: Promote sturdy branches that bear abundant nuts. Open crown to let in light.
HOW TO PRUNE: Train to a central leader, removing lower limbs over a period of three years so you can walk under the tree. Remove rubbing branches, leaving those that join the trunk at a wide angle. If necessary, thin crown of mature trees to let in light.
WHEN: Summer or mid- to late fall.
TIP: Will bleed if pruned when sap is rising in late winter or early spring.

KOELREUTERIA PANICULATA

Goldenrain tree

GOAL: Develop a strong structural framework and maintain wide-branching natural form.
HOW TO PRUNE: Select strong, well-spaced scaffold branches on young tree. Little other pruning needed. Thin occasionally to maintain graceful form and to remove dead limbs.
WHEN: Winter.
TIP: Don't prune hard or cut back tips of branches.

LABURNUM X WATERERI

Goldenchain tree

GOAL: Develop a strong structural framework, encourage natural vase shape, and remove seed pods, which are poisonous.
HOW TO PRUNE: Over a period of three to four years, remove limbs closer to ground than 6 or 7 feet. Develop central leader.
WHEN: Prune after flowering.
TIP: Will bleed if pruned in early spring. Regular pruning when young avoids large cuts, which close slowly, later on.

Goldenchain tree

LARIX

Larches

GOAL: Develop a strong structural framework and limit spread yet maintain natural pyramidal form.
HOW TO PRUNE: Develop central leader. Pinch tips of branches to encourage denser growth and to subdue wide spreading habit.
WHEN: Pinch in late spring, after growth has started. Do other pruning anytime.
TIP: Larches are deciduous conifers. European larch (*L. decidua*) has a pyramidal shape when young and broadens as it matures.

LIQUIDAMBAR STYRACIFLUA

Sweetgum, red gum

GOAL: Establish a strong central leader and maintain natural form.
HOW TO PRUNE: Choose widely-spaced scaffold branches. Remove extra-long growth. Little other pruning required.
WHEN: Winter.
TIP: Sweetgum has a pyramidal shape when young but becomes more rounded as it matures.

LIRIODENDRON TULIPIFERA

Tulip tree, tulip poplar

GOAL: Develop a central leader and maintain natural form.
HOW TO PRUNE: Train to a central leader. Remove crossing branches and upright shoots.
WHEN: Winter.
TIP: Large cuts close slowly. Tulip poplars are susceptible to lightning strikes, so avoid planting them near the house.

MACLURA POMIFERA

Osage orange

GOAL: Encourage a central leader when young and maintain the broad crown of the mature tree.
HOW TO PRUNE: Train to a central leader. Otherwise, little pruning is necessary.
WHEN: Winter.
TIP: Wear gloves when pruning to avoid thorns and harmful milky sap. Broad crown develops as tree matures. The dense wood quickly dulls pruning saws.

Saucer magnolia

MAGNOLIA

Magnolias, cucumber trees

GOAL: Develop a strong structural framework, maintain irregular to broad-spreading natural form, and show off attractive flowers and bark.
HOW TO PRUNE: Remove lower branches and leave several leaders to create a multi-trunked tree or only one leader for a single-trunked tree. Remove crossing branches. Train to four or five main scaffold branches that begin about 1 foot above the ground. Thin as necessary.
WHEN: After flowering.
TIP: See the evergreen trees chapter for southern magnolia and the deciduous shrubs chapter for star, lily, and Loebners magnolias.

MALUS

Crabapples

GOAL: Develop a strong open framework and keep trees thinned so that air and light can penetrate the interior.
HOW TO PRUNE: Train to modified central leader (see the chapter on fruit, page 88). Remove suckers, water sprouts, and dead and crossing branches. Thin neglected trees over a period of three or four years.
WHEN: After flowering but before early June when flower buds start to form.
TIP: Browned leaves and stems bent like shepherd's crooks are signs of fireblight. Cut back 6 to 12 inches into healthy tissue and disinfect tools between each cut. Infrequent pruning, in which you remove many limbs, leads to water sprouts and reduced flowering.

ENCYCLOPEDIA OF DECIDUOUS TREES
continued

MELIA AZEDARACH

Chinaberry

GOAL: Develop a strong structural framework.
HOW TO PRUNE: Train to a central leader and remove limbs on bottom 6 feet of trunk to encourage dense branching in canopy. Little other pruning required.
WHEN: Fall.

METASEQUOIA GLYPTOSTROBOIDES

Dawn redwood

GOAL: Develop and maintain a natural pyramidal form.
HOW TO PRUNE: Little pruning necessary.
WHEN: Winter.
TIP: Dawn redwood is a deciduous conifer. Cut a branch only as far back as the leaves grow. Branches without leaves will not regrow.

Dawn redwood

NYSSA SYLVATICA

Black gum, black tupelo

GOAL: Maintain an upright, pyramidal shape.
HOW TO PRUNE: Train to a central leader. Remove dead and crossing branches. Because branches are pendulous, remove enough lower limbs over four or five years that you can walk under the tree.
WHEN: Winter.
TIP: Control height by heading tree back when it reaches 20 feet.

Black gum

OSTRYA VIRGINIANA

American hop hornbeam

GOAL: Develop a strong structural framework and develop and maintain a graceful rounded habit with horizontal to drooping branching.
HOW TO PRUNE: Train to a central leader. Over a period of five years, remove lower limbs to a height of 6 to 8 feet. Remove witches brooms, twiggy masses that look like a broom.
WHEN: Fall.

OXYDENDRUM ARBOREUM

Sourwood

GOAL: Develop a strong structural framework, as well as develop and maintain a graceful narrow shape.
HOW TO PRUNE: Train to a central leader and remove narrow crotches.
WHEN: Winter.
TIP: Leave lower limbs on young tree to strengthen the trunk. Sourwood has a narrow shape when young, with the top becoming gradually rounded.

PARROTIA PERSICA

Persian parrotia

GOAL: Develop a strong framework and reveal interesting bark.
HOW TO PRUNE: Train to a single trunk and shorten side branches to encourage tree form. When tree reaches the height you want, prune off one-third of the lower branches each year for three years. Remove suckers that may develop.
WHEN: Winter.

PAULOWNIA TOMENTOSA

Princess tree, royal paulownia, empress tree

GOAL: Develop a strong framework with branches starting at least 5 feet off the ground and remove dead, damaged, and diseased limbs as often as necessary.
HOW TO PRUNE: Maintain a central leader. Rub out lower buds so limbs don't develop below 5 feet.
WHEN: Winter or early spring or after flowering.
TIP: For a tropical look, prune back hard each year to produce giant leaves and a mass of foliage. This eliminates flowers and reduces the amount of shade the tree casts.

PHELLODENDRON AMURENSE

Amur corktree

GOAL: Develop a strong structural framework and maintain a rounded form with a horizontal branching pattern.
HOW TO PRUNE: Train to a single leader with branches beginning 5 feet above the ground. Little other pruning is needed except for regular grooming.
WHEN: Winter.

Chinese pistachio

PISTACIA CHINENSIS

Chinese pistachio

GOAL: Develop a strong structural framework and maintain a natural rounded form.
HOW TO PRUNE: Train to a central leader with widely-spaced scaffold branches. Remove limbs that grow downward and those that form narrow crotches. On mature trees, remove dead branches and thin or prune laterally to reduce weight on scaffolds.
WHEN: Winter.

PLATANUS X ACERIFOLIA

Sycamore, London planetree

GOAL: Develop a strong framework and show off bark.
HOW TO PRUNE: Develop a central leader with wide-angled scaffold branches. Over three or four years, prune off lower limbs to a height of 8 to 12 feet. Remove dead and crossing branches as well as narrow crotches.
WHEN: Winter.
TIP: This tree is sometimes pollarded.

POPULUS

Poplars, cottonwoods, aspens

GOAL: Develop a strong framework, remove dead and damaged limbs and root suckers, display aspen bark, and encourage branching from the base of columnar trees.
HOW TO PRUNE: Cut root suckers back to the ground. Remove lower limbs of quaking aspen (*P. tremuloides*) to reveal bark. If needed, head back young columnar cultivars to about 6 inches above the ground so they will branch from the base. Cottonwood (*P. deltoides*) needs little pruning, except for removing dead and damaged limbs.
WHEN: Early to midwinter.
TIP: Will bleed if pruned in spring.

PRUNUS

Flowering plum, almond, apricot, cherry

GOAL: Establish a strong framework; remove dead, rubbing, or crossing branches; show off bark; and encourage natural form.
HOW TO PRUNE: Train to a central leader with widely-spaced scaffolds. Remove crossing branches and water sprouts or suckers. Over three or four years, prune off lower limbs on nonweeping forms. Remove upright branches on weeping cherries.
WHEN: After flowering. Remove diseased branches whenever found.
TIP: Inspect frequently for black-knot fungus and remove limb if found. Fruiting species are covered in the chapter on fruit, page 88.

PSEUDOLARIX KAEMPFERI

Golden larch

GOAL: Maintain a strong central leader and natural form.
HOW TO PRUNE: Pinch tips to promote bushiness while the tree is still small. Train to a central leader with wide-angled crotches. On older branches, cut back only into areas that still have foliage.
WHEN: Pinch in late spring. Other pruning may be done anytime.
TIP: Golden larch is a deciduous conifer. Its branches sweep almost to the ground.

Golden larch

ENCYCLOPEDIA OF DECIDUOUS TREES
continued

PYRUS

Ornamental pears

GOAL: Develop a strong framework that reduces limb breakage and splitting and remove dead, damaged, and diseased limbs as often as necessary.
HOW TO PRUNE: Train young trees to a central leader with evenly spaced wide-angled scaffold branches. Remove limbs with narrow crotch angles, upright and crossing branches, and crowded limbs. Remove suckers.
WHEN: After flowering.
TIP: Some species are subject to fireblight. Cut back infected tissue 6 to 12 inches into healthy tissue and disinfect pruning tools between each cut.

QUERCUS

Oaks

GOAL: Develop a strong central leader.
HOW TO PRUNE: Train to a central leader with well-spaced and wide-angled scaffold branches. Select high scaffolds on pin oak (*Q. palustris*) because lower branches grow downward. Remove crossing or damaged branches. Little pruning needed on most oaks.
WHEN: Late winter or early spring. Where oak wilt is a problem, don't prune in April through June.
TIP: California live oak and southern live oak are listed in the encyclopedia of evergreen trees.

ROBINIA PSEUDOACACIA

Black locust

GOAL: Develop a strong structural framework and prevent wind damage.
HOW TO PRUNE: Train to a central leader with wide-spaced scaffold limbs. Remove suckers and damaged branches. Thin crown to reduce weight and decrease wind damage.
WHEN: Mid- to late summer to avoid bleeding.
TIP: Wear thorn-proof gloves and long sleeves when pruning.

'Bradford' pear

SALIX BABYLONICA

Weeping willow

GOAL: Develop a strong structure, remove dead wood, and maintain weeping form.
HOW TO PRUNE: Train to a central leader and remove branches below 10 to 15 feet over a period of three to four years. Remove dead or damaged limbs. Trim branches so they don't sweep the ground.
WHEN: Winter or anytime.

SASSAFRAS ALBIDUM

Sassafras

GOAL: Develop and maintain a natural form.
HOW TO PRUNE: Train to central leader and remove limbs lower than 8 feet over a period of three to four years to expose interesting bark. Remove suckers.
WHEN: Winter.

SOPHORA JAPONICA

Japanese pagoda tree

GOAL: Develop a strong framework and remove dead wood.
HOW TO PRUNE: Train to a central leader with well-spaced scaffolds that join the trunk at wide angles. Thin or laterally prune as necessary to lessen weight on lower branches.
WHEN: Summer.
TIP: Bleeds if pruned in spring.

Mountain ash

SORBUS

Mountain ashes

GOAL: Develop a strong structure and remove fireblight damage quickly.
HOW TO PRUNE: Train to a central leader with wide-angled scaffold branches. Remove crossing limbs.
WHEN: Winter.
TIP: Fireblight can be a problem. If present, prune 6 to 12 inches into healthy tissue and disinfect tools between each cut. Mountain ash has a narrow shape when young and becomes more rounded as it ages.

STEWARTIA

Stewartias

GOAL: Develop a strong structural framework, maintain form, and display bark.
HOW TO PRUNE: Develop a central leader, otherwise let tree grow naturally. Little other pruning needed.
WHEN: Winter.
TIP: Some species are shrublike.

TAXODIUM DISTICHUM

Bald cypress

GOAL: Develop a strong structural framework and maintain pyramidal shape.
HOW TO PRUNE: Train to a central leader and remove crossing branches. To encourage bushier growth, pinch new shoots in spring. Remove lower limbs as needed.
WHEN: Winter.
TIP: Bald cypress is a deciduous conifer. It leafs out late in spring. Cut a branch only as far back as the leaves grow. Branches without leaves will not regrow.

TILIA

Lindens

GOAL: Maintain pyramidal shape and thin to remove interior crowding.
HOW TO PRUNE: Train to a central leader with wide-angled scaffold branches. Remove crowded limbs, multiple branches that develop from the same spot on the trunk, and root suckers.
WHEN: Late winter or early spring.
TIP: Basswood (*T. americana*) has a rounded head. Silver linden (*T. tomentosa*) is pyramidal when young but develops an upright oval form at maturity. Littleleaf linden (*T. cordata*) grows in a pyramidal shape that becomes slightly rounded with age. Suckers can be a problem on lindens.

ULMUS

Elms

GOAL: Develop a strong structural framework. For American elm (*U. americana*), remove dying and broken branches, which attract elm bark beetles which carry Dutch elm disease, and maintain the vase shape. Develop a strong structure for Siberian elm (*U. pumila*). Show off bark of lacebark elm (*U. parvifolia*).
HOW TO PRUNE: Tolerates pruning but rarely needs it. Train to a central leader and promptly remove crossing, damaged, or diseased branches. Thin lacebark elm yearly to avoid crowded crown; remove branches below 8 feet over a period of three to four years to exhibit bark. Train Siberian elm so that it has wide-angled scaffold branches. Thin canopy to reduce wind resistance, if necessary. Remove broken branches.
WHEN: Late winter or early spring. Do not prune American elm in late spring or early summer because that is when elm bark beetles are active.
TIP: Siberian elm has weak branches that often break in high winds or under the weight of snow. The tree can "bleed" in spring.

ZELKOVA SERRATA

Japanese or sawleaf zelkova

GOAL: Develop a strong, natural shape and highlight attractive mottled bark.
HOW TO PRUNE: Maintain a single trunk and thin the crown so it does not become crowded. Select wide-spaced scaffolds.
WHEN: Winter.
TIP: Round-headed as a young tree; matures to a vase shape.

PRUNING DECIDUOUS SHRUBS AND VINES

Although mature deciduous trees can get by with infrequent pruning, established shrubs may need pruning at least once a year to either control size or maintain vigor. Also, unlike trees, where only thinning cuts are recommended, shrubs might also require heading and shearing, depending upon your goal for the shrub. You may want to review these pruning techniques, which are described in the first chapter.

Before picking up your pruners, always have a goal in mind and know which type of pruning cut produces the effect you want. You may want to maintain a shrub's natural form or create a hedge, topiary, or espalier. Other typical goals include:

CONTROLLING SIZE: When shrubs grow too large, use thinning cuts to reduce size without changing the natural branching habit. First, remove excessive twiggy growth and crowded, weak, and misshapen stems, as well as suckers and water sprouts. Then use loppers to cut the longest stems back to where they join a lateral branch. This opens the plant to sunlight, which encourages new growth and gives it a graceful shape. If you shear or head a shrub to control size, you'll get a fast flush of growth that requires more pruning—exactly the opposite of what you want.

Two other methods of reducing the size of a shrub are explained on page 36.

ENCOURAGING THICKER GROWTH: A shrub that is grown to screen off an unsightly view needs to be dense, not loose and open. In this situation, greater branching and thicker growth are what you want, so shearing or heading is appropriate. You can also control the size of such plants with lateral cuts.

PROMOTING FLOWERS: When a shrub isn't blooming as well as it has in the past, the first thing to check is whether it's still receiving enough sunshine. As surrounding trees grow, they'll gradually shade an area. If the light hasn't become too dim to support the plant, thinning the shrub's older branches can help. Thinning lets light into the interior of the shrub to help stimulate growth and improve flowering.

Beauty bush flowers on the previous season's growth. Cut about one-third of the canes to the ground each year to ensure plentiful fruit.

SHRUB SHAPES

Weeping

Spreading

Prostrate

SPRING-FLOWERING SHRUBS

Late winter

Early spring

Late spring

Summer

Leaf and flower buds are developed and ready to go.

Blooms appear first, but leaves may open, too.

Prune these shrubs as soon as flowers fade.

Next year's flower buds develop on the new stems.

SUMMER-FLOWERING SHRUBS

Late winter

Early spring

Late spring

Summer

In spring, leaf buds are there but not flower buds.

Prune the shrub before it starts growing.

Each cut results in at least two new branches.

The new branches produce a wealth of blooms.

If light is not the problem, make sure you're pruning the shrubs at the correct time. For example, trimming a weigela or other spring bloomer in September removes most of the buds that would flower the next spring. Wait to prune shrubs that bloom on old or previous season's wood until after flowering is over. Prune shrubs that bloom on new or current-season wood before they bloom in late winter or early spring to stimulate new growth on which flowers develop. If you're hoping for berries, remember, flowers produce the berries.

For specifics, find your shrub in the encyclopedia, beginning on page 44, or check the box on page 13 for some guidelines on timing.

REMOVING REVERTING FOLIAGE: On variegated shrubs—the ones with mottled foliage—cut out any branches with green leaves that develop. If you don't, the entire shrub may revert to green as the stronger green sports shade out the variegated branches. If fast-growing sprouts appear on dwarf varieties, cut them out, too.

AGE MAKES A DIFFERENCE

Before deciding to prune a shrub, consider its age and vigor. Older, less vigorous, shrubs should be pruned more lightly than younger ones, unless you are pruning to rejuvenate. Then you can prune the older shrub's branches back to the ground.

Don't wait until a shrub has outgrown its site to begin pruning or training. Start when it is young so it will develop a compact branching system. Lightly head limbs of small shrubs to encourage branching at the base of the plant. Then thin the shrub to make sure the basal branches are evenly spaced.

Upright

Rounded

Oval

REJUVENATING SHRUBS

Rejuvenating a shrub is a three-year process. Each year, remove one-third of the oldest stems at ground level to end up with a naturally shaped plant.

When faced with neglected or overgrown shrubs, homeowners often feel helpless. They wonder whether the only solution is digging them out and replacing them with new plants. But such shrubs can be given a new lease on life through one of three renovation techniques. Within three years, they will be back in shape, flowering better than before. A little patience pays off in the end.

HOW TO TURN A LARGE SHRUB INTO A SMALL TREE

Start by selecting one to three stems to be the main trunk (or trunks) and remove all other stems. Expose the trunks by cutting off the side limbs up to where you'd like the tree canopy to begin—usually about 4 to 6 feet, although it can be shorter on some shrubs. Continue to remove side shoots as they appear. Sprouting will lessen over time. Or, you can treat the shrub with a growth regulator.

GRADUAL RENEWAL

This method takes a bit longer to see results, but it's easy on the shrubs, and it doesn't create a temporary eyesore. Each year for three years, cut one-third of the oldest stems off at ground level, using loppers or a folding saw. The result is a "new" shrub with a pleasing natural shape and a size that fits the spot where it's planted. Some gardeners like to perform renewal pruning over five years instead of three, taking out one-fifth of the stems each year. After the plant has been through this process, keep its size under control with yearly thinning.

SEVERE PRUNING

Another good way to renovate shrubs is to cut all of the stems back to within 1 to 2 inches of the ground. On a shrub with heavy branches, you may want to make two cuts— first remove the top growth with loppers, then cut the thick stem base with a saw.

When a shrub has been cut back hard, it won't look attractive for a year, but generally it will regrow very quickly. This is often the best way to treat a shrub, such as viburnum, that was sheared by a previous owner rather than allowed to grow into a natural shape.

A caution: Not all shrubs respond well to this treatment. It works best for vigorous growers, such as forsythia, glossy abelia, and spirea. See the shrub encyclopedia for others that tolerate heavy or hard pruning.

TRANSFORMING A SHRUB INTO A TREE

Another solution to the problem of overgrown deciduous shrubs is to turn the shrub into a single- or multiple-trunk tree. This technique—often used on crape myrtles—produces a shrub that has a light, airy look to it and opens areas at the base for planting ground covers or flowers. See the box at left for how-to directions.

WHEN TO RENOVATE A SHRUB

The best time to prune is in early spring before new growth begins because the plants recover quickly then. You can wait until after flowering to rejuvenate a shrub, but regrowth will be more vigorous in early spring.

PRUNING ROSES

Correct pruning of hybrid tea roses (above) and climbing roses (right) results in an attractive form and showy, abundant flowers.

More so than with other shrubs, it's easy to see quick results from pruning roses. Not only do correctly pruned roses produce more flowers, but they're also healthier and have a more pleasing shape.

PRUNING AT PLANTING

It is rarely necessary to prune bare-root rosebushes when planting them. Ordinarily, the grower has already done this. But if stems or roots were damaged in transit, clip those off with a sharp pair of pruners.

ESTABLISHED ROSES

How and when a rose is pruned depends upon its type—hybrid tea, floribunda, climber, grandiflora, rambler, miniature, shrub, or old garden rose. See the step-by-step illustrations on pages 38 and 39 for specifics.

PRUNE ANYTIME: Some tasks apply to all roses: removing dead, diseased, weak, crossing, or damaged stems, and cutting off suckers from below the bud union (grafting site).

PRUNE AS YOU CUT FLOWERS: Some pruning is also done throughout the summer as you deadhead or snip off blooms to enjoy indoors. Cut ¼ inch above the next five-leaflet cluster below the blossom. Choose a cluster that's facing the outside of the plant. Don't leave faded flowers on the bush because they slow the formation of new blooms.

LATE WINTER OR SPRING: When's the best time to do major pruning of hybrid teas, floribundas, polyanthas, grandifloras, miniatures, and tree roses? It depends upon where you live.

In cold climates, prune in early spring, as soon as the buds have begun to swell but before new growth has started. Be careful though: Late frosts can kill new growth.

In mild climates, late winter is an ideal time to prune. But in areas where spring temperatures waver between 30° and 70° F, wait to prune until 30 days before the average last frost to avoid exposing new growth to a killing cold spell.

With an old garden rose, shrub rose, rambler, or climber, pruning time depends upon whether it blooms on this year's or last year's canes. If the flowers are on the tips of the stems, your plant blooms on new canes. If the roses are a bit farther down the stem, it probably blooms on last year's canes.

PRUNING ROSES
continued

In early spring, prune roses that bloom on this year's canes, such as hybrid teas, grandifloras, and floribundas. Wait until after flowering to prune roses that bloom on older wood (many species roses). However, don't prune climbers or ramblers until they're at least three years old, except to remove diseased or damaged canes.

Old garden roses frequently need only minimal pruning. Remove one-third of the oldest canes—they'll be brown or black—of alba, centifolia, and moss roses after they finish flowering. Prune China, Bourbon, Portland, and modern shrub roses in the same manner in late winter or early spring.

Miniature roses need only minimal pruning. If it's necessary, prune them as you would hybrid teas. You can also shear them with hedge pruners to increase bushiness.

LIGHT AND HEAVY PRUNING

Roses that bloom on current-year wood respond well to heavy and light pruning. When pruning heavy—or hard—you remove all but three to five of the plant's canes and head remaining canes to three buds. This method produces larger flowers but fewer of them. It also stimulates new growth on weak bushes.

Light pruning has the opposite result: more and smaller flowers. With light pruning, you remove all but five to seven canes, cutting remaining canes to 18 to 36 inches tall.

Gardeners in cold climates are more likely than those in warm climates to have to prune back hard because of winter damage. But if there's a choice, inexperienced rose growers should choose light to moderate pruning rather than cutting back hard. A general rule for hybrid teas, grandifloras, polyanthas, and miniatures is to remove only one-third to one-half of the plant's growth.

THE BUD UNION

The knob at the base of the canes is the bud union. This is where one variety of rose was grafted to the root system of another. Usually, the rootstock is a strong grower; however, because of its vigor, canes may develop from below the bud union. These canes grow robustly and will take over if not removed. They also produce inferior flowers that may not be the same color as the desired variety. If, for example, a red rose appears among the yellow ones, trace that cane back to its origin and cut it off.

TIPS

WHEN TO STOP: In areas with cold winters, quit pruning four to six weeks before the average first fall frost date. Pruning later may promote late growth and winter injury.
TECHNIQUE: Cut at a 45-degree angle ¼ inch above an outward-facing bud. Wear a pair of long, thorn-proof gloves as you work.
SEALING: Many gardeners seal the tips of the canes to prevent borers from damaging them. In warm climates, cover all cuts—even those from deadheading—with Elmer's glue, shellac, fingernail polish, or special rose-pruning sealants. In cold climates, seal ½-inch-diameter or larger cuts.

A light pruning of dormant hybrid tea roses leaves five to seven canes about 18 inches tall.

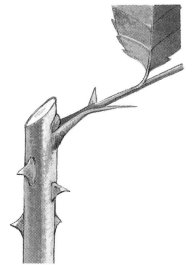

Make all cuts at a 45 degree angle ¼ inch above an outward facing bud. Angle cuts away from buds.

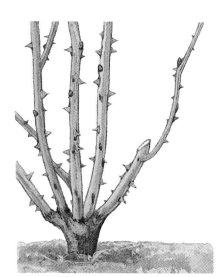

Pruning to an outward-facing bud directs the new stem to the outside and maintains the rose's shape.

Ramblers are climbing roses that bloom prolifically on year-old wood. Shoots need to be carefully trained and controlled or a tangled mess results. Prune them after they finish flowering.

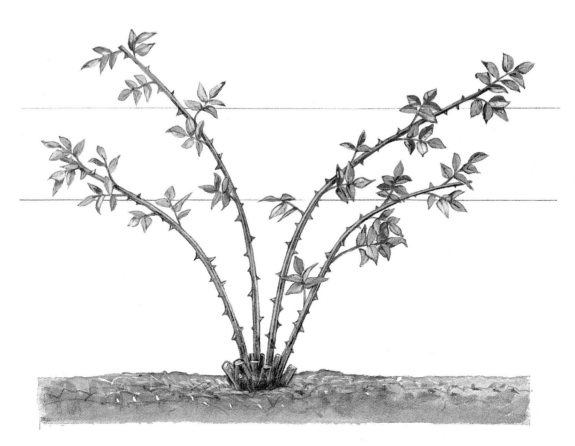

Remove the canes that flowered as well as scrawny branches, retaining 4 to 5 of the most vigorous new canes spaced evenly apart. For the most abundant bloom, tie the canes to a fence or trellis so they grow horizontally or in a fan shape.

HEDGES

Hedges are typically sheared for a formal look. To maintain the look, lightly shear them with a hedge trimmer a few times during the growing season. For a flowering formal hedge pay attention to timing and use lateral pruning cuts.

An informal hedge of a deciduous flowering shrub offers striking foliage and an array of flowers. Thin a portion of the oldest branches and stems annually for uniform growth.

How you prune your hedge depends upon whether it's formal or informal. A formal hedge has straight sides and a flat top or other geometrical shape. To keep it looking good requires frequent light shearing. An informal hedge, which grows to its natural form, needs less maintenance. Informal hedges that flower are given their main pruning of the year right after they bloom.

TRAINING A YOUNG HEDGE

The treatment you give your hedge the first few years after planting makes a big difference in how it looks and grows in the long run. Within a month after planting, head the young nursery stock by one-third to one-half.

People are often reluctant to prune these small, young shrubs that have so recently been planted. True, early pruning will make the young plants smaller temporarily, but more importantly, it encourages the development of many new stems from the existing stems, resulting in a thicker hedge, especially at its base. If young hedge plants are allowed to grow unpruned until they reach their intended height, the inner growth will be weak, and branching will occur only at the tips of the stems. The hedge won't be

Shear off new growth whenever the hedge has grown about 2 to 3 inches. You will find it helpful to run a guideline along the hedge between two stakes to keep the top of the hedge level.

Training a hedge so that the sides angle in correctly can be tricky. One solution is to make a guide from 1×1s. Cut the legs slightly taller than the hedge; the top slightly wider. Join the pieces with wing nuts to adjust the angle.

dense enough to support weight, and snow or strong winds can break the weak branches, which will leave holes in the hedge.

SHEARING AND SHAPING

FORMAL HEDGES: In the spring of a formal hedge's second and third years, use hedge trimmers to level its top and sides. Each time there's 2 to 3 inches of new growth, clip it back just above the previous trimming.

Part of the training of young formal hedges is to shape them so the bottom is wider than the top. If you prune the opposite way, the top shades the base, which eventually grows bare. One way to maintain a base that's wider than the top is to begin shearing at the bottom, then work up, tapering the sides.

Shearing long formal hedges is easier with gas, electric, or battery-powered hedge trimmers. Manual hedge shears work fine for shorter hedges. Hand pruners are best for hedges made up of broadleaf shrubs because, unlike trimmers, they allow you to avoid clipping the wide leaves in half, which spoils the appearance of the hedge.

It isn't easy to shear a formal hedge to an exactly straight edge by eye. To get the angles correct, set up stakes at each end of the hedge and stretch string between them as a guide.

Once the plant is established, shear before growth begins in spring so that the new leaves cover the pruning cuts. You can also shear during or after the first growth spurt. Stop trimming in late summer—August or

September—or early enough that the new growth isn't damaged by early cold spells.

INFORMAL HEDGES: Informal hedges offer much more leeway with your schedule: Most shrubs can be thinned any time of the year. Let them grow without pruning through their second season, except to remove broken or diseased branches.

Hand pruners or loppers are recommended for pruning informal hedges because you use thinning and lateral cuts to remove branches and allow sunlight into the center of a shrub.

RENOVATING A HEDGE

When a hedge becomes overgrown or bare at the bottom, it needs rejuvenating. Some hedges rebound quickly if cut back to within 2 or 3 inches of the ground. This works well with vigorous deciduous species such as privet, bayberry, and spirea, as well as with some broadleaf evergreens such as holly and boxwood. This will not work with needled evergreens because they will not regrow from bare branches.

Cutting a hedge back to a few inches high temporarily destroys its screening ability. For that reason, you may prefer to rejuvenate a hedge over three years, cutting one-third of the stems to the ground each year.

While a hedge is being renovated, it won't look very good. But within two years of severe pruning and three to four years of gradual rejuvenation, its appearance will be better than before you started.

VINES

Vines are pruned for the same reasons that deciduous shrubs are—to contain their size, improve flowering, and remove weak or dead growth. The techniques used are similar, as is the timing.

WHEN TO PRUNE

Prune vines that bloom on the current season's growth in early spring, just before they begin to grow. Wait until after flowering to prune vines that bloom on the previous year's growth. Then you won't sacrifice any of the show. Pruning an overly aggressive vine, such as wisteria, in summer tends to slow its growth.

Clematis is divided into three groups, with different times to prune each, so it's best to check the vine encyclopedia for more details on when and how to prune this popular flowering vine.

PRUNING AT PLANTING

Gardeners are sometimes horrified when told to cut back their newly planted vine by half or more, but that's what it takes to get it off to a good start. For vigorous new growth, thin the vine to one or two main stems and two or three of the strongest side shoots.

ESTABLISHED VINES

Once a vine has grown into the spot allotted for it, most of your pruning will be to trim back any shoots that have been damaged by weather or insects, or that grow out of bounds. Also promptly cut out dead, diseased, or weak stems as well as all suckers. When these remain, the vine looks messy.

Vines, like shrubs, are pruned using all the main pruning cuts—thinning, heading, and pinching, which are described in the first chapter. Use thinning cuts to remove crowded growth.

Vines that grow on current season's wood should be cut back to a basic framework in winter, leaving two or three buds on the stem. Prune those that bloom on old wood after they finish flowering.

Fast-growing vines, such as this 'Blue Dancer' clematis, need some type of structure to support them and show off their flowers.

To encourage branching on leggy stems, head them back. Each year, cut vines that flower on new stems almost to the ground. Also cut any vine that has grown bare at the bottom to 2 or 3 inches tall.

When a portion of a clinging vine (one that uses adhesive pads to adhere to a surface) comes loose, cut it off at a bud below the unattached part. This is necessary because it will not refasten to the wall.

AGGRESSIVE VINES

Vines that are especially vigorous need hard pruning several times a year to keep them from taking over. These include wisteria, trumpet vine, and Japanese honeysuckle. Prune them once in the dormant season and several times during the summer. Keep growth

TRAINING AN ESPALIER

Is it a shrub, a tree, or a vine? It's an espalier: a shrub or tree that's trained to look like a vine growing against a wall in a symmetrical pattern. Either deciduous or evergreen shrubs are suitable for espalier. The only requirement is that their branches be flexible; avoid shrubs that are stiff and upright.

Some good choices for espaliering are pyracantha, viburnum, forsythia, cotoneaster, yew, crabapple, atlas cedar, sweet bay, flowering quince, and figs. In cooler climates, dwarf apples and other fruit trees are espaliered, but the heat from a wall will be too hot for the plant to develop fruit in areas where summer temperatures often remain over 90° F.

While there are several shapes of espalier, one attractive one is called the double cordon. It has a central trunk with two tiers of horizontal branches. First, attach horizontal wires 18 inches apart on the wall. The wires should stand out 6–12 inches from the wall to allow air circulation behind the plant.

As you plant the shrub, clip its main stem to just above the bottom wire. New shoots will emerge from the cut. Select one to grow straight up to the second wire and choose two others to train along the bottom

TRAINING A CORDON ESPALIER

Start with a young, dormant, unbranched seedling. Trim its main stem to about 15 inches or the height of the bottom wire.

Select three of the stems that develop above the cut. Train the center one vertically. Tie the other two to a trellis at a 45-degree angle.

In winter, loosely tie the branches to the trellis. Pinch them to encourage lateral branching, cutting horizontal stems to a downward-facing bud.

wire in each direction. Rub off all other growth. In winter, tie the side branches to the trellis, spreading them horizontally. Prune them to 18 inches long, cutting to a downward-facing bud. Trim the upright stem just below the top wire to develop the second tier of side branches.

---

in check by shortening some of the stems each year, or prune them back to five or six buds during the dormant season.

OVERGROWN VINES

When a vine has grown into a huge tangle of stems, wait until late winter or early spring to renovate it. If it is on a support, remove the vine from its support and place it on the ground. Then cut out the old, woody stems, leaving one or two young stems at the base.

While this seems a radical approach, you'll be pleased when vigorous new growth begins

in spring. Just as with a new vine, keep only one or two main stems and several strong side shoots, pinching the tips of the shoots to encourage branching. To avoid having the vine become overgrown once again, prune it on a regular schedule, being especially attentive to thinning cuts.

Vines are sometimes used as ground covers. When these become overgrown, set the lawn mower blade as high as it will go and mow over the vine. This also prevents a mass of old stems from building up. However, don't wait until the ground cover becomes too deep to mow, as often happens with honeysuckle.

ENCYCLOPEDIA OF SHRUBS

ABUTILON

Flowering maples, Chinese lanterns

GOAL: Keep shrubs compact and in bounds, increase plant density, and encourage flowering.

HOW TO PRUNE: Cut flowering maple or Chinese lantern (*A. × hybridum*) back hard to force new growth from the base. Tip pinch for density. For hybrids, pinch new growth after plants have at least six leaves on a branch. Prune *A. vitifolium* very little, except to deadhead. Shorten previous year's growth on trailing abutilon (*A. megapotamicum*) by approximately one-third.

WHEN: Trailing abutilon: early to midspring; flowering maple and variegated flowering maple: early spring; *A. vitifolium*: after flowering.

TIP: Abutilons flower on the current season's growth.

AESCULUS PARVIFLORA

Bottlebrush buckeye

GOAL: Control suckering and size, yet maintain vigor.

HOW TO PRUNE: Remove one-third of the limbs at their base each year for three years. Use thinning cuts to preserve shrub form.

WHEN: Late winter.

TIP: Bottlebrush buckeye can be invasive. Suckers will eventually form a large thicket if some aren't removed by pruning.

Flowering maple

ARONIA ARBUTIFOLIA

Red chokeberry

GOAL: Encourage branching, decrease legginess, and maintain vigor.

HOW TO PRUNE: On mature shrub, cut one-third of old stems back to the ground every year. Dig up excess suckers. Chokeberry flowers on old wood.

WHEN: After berries have dropped.

TIP: An arching, spreading habit is natural for red chokeberry.

BAMBOOS

GOAL: Control size and spread.

HOW TO PRUNE: Shear back tops of dwarf bamboo and clump bamboo grown as a hedge. Thin running bamboo and giant bamboo by cutting three-year-old canes back to their base. For best appearance, remove lower side branches of giant bamboo. Keep running bamboo from spreading beyond its boundaries by root pruning, mowing, and installing a metal or concrete barrier 18 inches or more deep.

WHEN: Late spring.

TIP: Canes of bamboo often die if you cut below the leaves.

Red chokeberry

BERBERIS THUNBERGII

Japanese barberry

GOAL: Open crowded interior of the plant and maintain shape and vigor. Barberry can be sheared but it looks best when thinned.
HOW TO PRUNE: Thin as necessary to maintain shape and size. Pinch tips to induce bushiness. To renovate, cut one-third of old stems to the ground each year for three years. 'Crimson Pygmy' cultivar needs little pruning.
WHEN: Early spring. Pinch after shrub has flowered to enhance fruit.
TIP: For protection, wear long sleeves and thorn-proof gloves when pruning barberries.

BUDDLEJA

Butterfly bush, summer lilac, orange-eye buddleia

GOAL: Control size and flowering.
HOW TO PRUNE: Cut these fast-growing shrubs to 6 to 12 inches high to stimulate new growth. Flowers on new season's growth.
WHEN: Late winter or early spring.
TIP: Winter-killed shrubs usually grow back from roots. Rangy habit is natural.

Butterfly bush

CALLICARPA

Beautyberries

GOAL: Control size and encourage abundant berries.
HOW TO PRUNE: Cut one-third of stems back to the ground each year. To renovate an overgrown beautyberry, cut the whole shrub back to 3 inches high. If injured by cold, cut damaged shoots to a healthy bud. Thin shrubs as needed. Beautyberries flower on current year's growth.
WHEN: Early spring.

CALYCANTHUS FLORIDUS

Sweet shrub, Carolina allspice, spicebush, strawberry shrub

GOAL: Control size and shape. Shrub is scraggly and unkempt in wild.
HOW TO PRUNE: Little pruning required. Remove dead or weak growth. Rejuvenate overgrown shrubs by cutting a third of the oldest canes to the ground for three years. Pinch new growth in late spring or early summer to keep the shrub small. Occasionally thin and trim sweet shrub as necessary. Sweet shrub blooms on the current year's growth.
WHEN: Early spring.

Carolina allspice

CARAGANA ARBORESCENS

Siberian peashrub

GOAL: Encourage dense growth. Train as a small tree if desired.
HOW TO PRUNE: Remove dead stems. Pinch tips or prune lightly to encourage bushiness. The shrub flowers on second year's growth.
WHEN: Late spring or early summer.
TIP: Shear to encourage dense growth, but Siberian peashrub is not suited for neat, formal hedges.

CARYOPTERIS X CLANDONENSIS

Bluebeard

GOAL: Increase blooms and keep the shape compact so the shrub does not become floppy.
HOW TO PRUNE: Cut back to within 6 inches of the ground each year. Flowers on new wood.
WHEN: Late winter or early spring.
TIP: If killed to the ground in cold climates, remove dead stems.

ENCYCLOPEDIA OF SHRUBS
continued

CHAENOMELES

Flowering quince

GOAL: Avoid a tangled, trash-catching mess, encourage abundant flowering, and maintain the shrub's natural shape.
HOW TO PRUNE: Remove dead twigs and debris caught in branches. Thin the tangled center of older neglected shrubs by cutting one-fourth of oldest canes to the ground each year. To increase flowering, trim new stem growth to six leaves after plants bloom. To relieve congestion, remove crossing branches. Blooms on old wood.
WHEN: After flowering.

CLETHRA ALNIFOLIA

Summersweet

GOAL: Allow shrub to grow in its natural oval shape.
HOW TO PRUNE: Remove suckers and weak growth and cut approximately one-fourth of old canes back to their base yearly if growth isn't vigorous. Flowers on current year's growth.
WHEN: Late winter or early spring.

Japanese flowering quince

CORNUS

Tartarian, redosier, and blood twig dogwoods

GOAL: Encourage vigorous growth on stems and retain open branching at tips.
HOW TO PRUNE: Cut one-third of stems back to the ground annually. Responds well to heavy pruning. Flowers on current season's growth.
WHEN: Late winter or early spring.
TIP: Pruning promotes colorful new stems.

CORYLUS AVELLANA

European filbert, European hazel

GOAL: Maintain natural shape and promote formation of abundant catkins.
HOW TO PRUNE: This plant can be trained as a small tree or multi-trunked shrub. Multiple stems develop naturally. For a single trunk, when the shrub is young, select the strongest stem and remove suckers as they appear. If growing as a shrub, thin old wood each year. Prune suckers to keep shrub from getting too bushy. Remove dead or damaged stems on 'Contorta' (Harry Lauder's walking stick).
WHEN: Dormant season (late winter).
TIP: 'Contorta' especially grows many suckers. Carefully dig them up and plant elsewhere or discard.

Tartarian dogwood

Smoke tree

COTINUS COGGYGRIA

Smoke tree

GOAL: Maintain open, airy habit.
HOW TO PRUNE: Little pruning is required. Remove dead branches, trim long straggly stems, and control unkempt appearance. Flowers on two- to three-year-old wood.
WHEN: Early spring.
TIP: Extensive pruning leads to excessive growth, destroying the shrub's natural form.

COTONEASTER

Cotoneasters

GOAL: Maintain natural upright fountainlike shape and encourage formation of berries.
HOW TO PRUNE: Cut branches with sparse growth back to main stem or to ground. Remove dead wood and thin the shrubs annually. Rejuvenate an upright cotoneaster by cutting it back to 6 inches high.
WHEN: Late winter or early spring.
TIP: Susceptible to fireblight. When removing diseased area, cut 6 to 12 inches into healthy tissue and disinfect pruners between each cut.

CYTISUS

Broom
(also includes *Genista* and *Spartium* species)

GOAL: Control legginess and allow shrub to develop into its natural form while encouraging dense growth and preventing seed formation, which weakens plants.
HOW TO PRUNE: Pinch new growth back by two-thirds on young shrubs to encourage bushiness. Remove dead stems. Deadhead spent blooms. Avoid cutting into leafless stem tissue because it won't produce new growth.
WHEN: After flowering.

DEUTZIA

Deutzia

GOAL: Encourage vigorous new growth and avoid straggliness.
HOW TO PRUNE: Remove one-fourth of canes to the base annually on mature specimens. Rejuvenate every five years by cutting shrub to the ground. Cut flowering stems halfway to base. Flowers develop on last season's growth.
WHEN: After flowering.
TIP: Remove flowers damaged by late frost.

DIERVILLA SESSILIFOLIA

Southern bush honeysuckle

GOAL: Stimulate vigorous new growth and attractive bronze foliage.
HOW TO PRUNE: Prune hard, cutting back to just above a pair of buds approximately a foot from the ground. Control spread by removing suckers when they appear. When overgrown, cut stems back to their base or dig up the shrub and replant young, vigorous sections. Southern bush honeysuckle flowers on current season's growth.
WHEN: Prune in early spring when plant is still dormant.

Southern bush honeysuckle

ENCYCLOPEDIA OF SHRUBS

continued

Burning bush

EUONYMUS ALATUS

Burning bush, winged euonymus

GOAL: Maintain a natural rounded shape with horizontal branching.
HOW TO PRUNE: Little pruning is needed. For an informal look, pinch tips. Thin selectively every other year to maintain branching, rather than head back.
WHEN: Early spring.
TIP: Withstands heavy pruning.

EXOCHORDA RACEMOSA

Pearlbush

GOAL: Pearlbush can become leggy, so prune to keep in bounds and maintain compactness.
HOW TO PRUNE: Cut one-fourth of old stems to ground annually. Remove suckers. Flowers on previous year's growth.
WHEN: Has a tendency to become congested if not pruned immediately after flowering.

FORSYTHIA X INTERMEDIA

Border forsythia

GOAL: Maintain natural weeping shape, encourage abundant flowers, and avoid ungainly overgrowth.
HOW TO PRUNE: Cut one-third of stems back to their base annually. Remove suckers. To decrease size, laterally prune the tallest branches. Flowers on previous year's growth.
WHEN: After flowering.
TIP: Shearing decreases number of flowers unless timed right.

FOTHERGILLA MAJOR

Fothergilla

GOAL: Develop natural rounded form.
HOW TO PRUNE: Rarely needed unless shrub has outgrown its space.
WHEN: Late winter.

Dwarf fothergilla

FUCHSIA X HYBRIDA

Hardy fuchsia

GOAL: Control size and encourage bushiness.
HOW TO PRUNE: Prune back winter-killed growth to green wood. If no winter damage, prune side branches to their bottom bud. Flowers on current season's growth.
WHEN: In frost-free areas, prune in winter. In cold-winter regions, after new growth begins in spring.
TIP: Hardy fuchsia may be evergreen or semievergreen.

HAMAMELIS

Chinese witch hazel, hybrid witch hazel

GOAL: Maintain natural form, which varies from spreading to vase-shaped, depending on the species.
HOW TO PRUNE: Once plant reaches the height you prefer, thin it to keep it at that size. You can train witch hazel to a tree shape by selecting a central leader, pinching side growth, and removing the suckers. As the tree develops, remove lower limbs over a period of three years, then thin the crown to shape it. Keep pruning to a minimum with Chinese witch hazel.
WHEN: Late spring or summer. Cut branches in winter to force blooms indoors, if desired.

HIBISCUS SYRIACUS

Rose of Sharon

GOAL: Encourage new growth that will produce plenty of flowers.
HOW TO PRUNE: Cut out dead or diseased stems. Thin overgrown shrubs. Prune hard each spring for larger flowers. Left unpruned, the shrub produces small, but profuse, flowers.
WHEN: Spring.
TIP: Rose of Sharon blooms on current season's growth.

Rose of Sharon

HYDRANGEA

Bigleaf, peegee, smooth, and oakleaf hydrangeas

GOAL: Maintain natural shape and encourage abundant flowering. Also increase the density of bigleaf hydrangea (*H. macrocarpa*), which tends to grow thin and woody but with an umbrella of foliage.
HOW TO PRUNE: Bigleaf hydrangea flowers on previous year's growth. Cut back stems that have flowered to about 2 feet tall or cut in half on dwarf species. Rejuvenate bigleaf hydrangea by cutting to the ground. Peegee hydrangea (*H. paniculata*) flowers on new growth. Remove most of its previous season's growth. Prune back smooth hydrangea (*H. arborescens*) to approximately 12 inches tall. Oakleaf hydrangea (*H. quercifolia*) requires very little pruning.
WHEN: Bigleaf hydrangea: immediately after flowering; peegee hydrangea: in early spring; smooth hydrangea: in late winter; oakleaf hydrangea, in early spring.

Hydrangea

HYPERICUM

St. John's wort

GOAL: Encourage new growth and flowering and maintain shape.
HOW TO PRUNE: Remove weak growth and cut up to one-fourth of stems back to the ground to encourage vigorous growth. Flowers on current growth.
WHEN: Spring.
TIP: Some species are evergreen.

ILEX

Deciduous holly, winterberry, possumhaw, yaupon

GOAL: Control size and vigor and enhance berries.
HOW TO PRUNE: If shrub is too large, cut one-third of its old stems back to the ground yearly. Otherwise, pruning isn't needed. Thin to rejuvenate shrubs.
WHEN: Early spring.
TIP: Withstands severe pruning. Most hollies are evergreen.

ITEA VIRGINICA

Virginia sweetspire

GOAL: Maintain informal shape, increase density, and keep colonies in check.
HOW TO PRUNE: Little required.
WHEN: After flowering.

ENCYCLOPEDIA OF SHRUBS
continued

Japanese kerria

KERRIA JAPONICA

Japanese kerria

GOAL: Encourage new growth, which has the best bright green color, and an abundant crop of blooms.
HOW TO PRUNE: Remove unwanted suckers and dead stems. Cut one-third of stems that have flowered to the ground each year for best flower production.
WHEN: After flowering.
TIP: Dieback of tips is normal; snip them off in spring.

KOLKWITZIA AMABILIS

Beauty bush

GOAL: Maintain arching form of beautybush without allowing the shrub to get leggy.
HOW TO PRUNE: Cut stems that have flowered back to their base. Flowers grow on previous season's growth. Rejuvenate to prevent bare lower limbs by cutting all stems to the ground.
WHEN: After flowering.

LAGERSTROEMIA INDICA

Crape myrtle

GOAL: Control shape and encourage maximum flowering.
HOW TO PRUNE: When pruning to control size of tall specimens, use lateral pruning cuts. For dwarfs, cut stems back to 4 inches tall. A heavy pruning encourages blooming. Flowers on current season's growth. Avoid topping. Remove twiggy growth and spent flowers in summer.
WHEN: In zones 6 and 7: spring. Remove winter-killed branches. In warmer regions: late winter.
TIP: Remove faded flowers. Train taller cultivars as trees by removing lower side branches; this shows off mottled bark.

LESPEDEZA THUNBERGII

Shrub bush clover

GOAL: Encourage new growth and keep shrub from becoming unkempt.
HOW TO PRUNE: Cut back to ground.
WHEN: In warm-winter areas, early spring. In cooler regions, wait until after chance of frost has passed.
TIP: Flowers form on current season's growth.

LIGUSTRUM

Privets

GOAL: Shape and keep in bounds.
HOW TO PRUNE: Shear privets grown as hedges. Thin individual shrubs in the landscape when they become crowded by removing one-fourth of oldest canes to the base over four years.
WHEN: Late winter or right after flowering. Shear hedges during summer.
TIP: Some privets are evergreen or semievergreen. Overgrown plants will tolerate heavy rejuvenation pruning.

LINDERA

Spicebushes

GOAL: Maintain rounded form.
HOW TO PRUNE: Remove winter-killed branches or tips of branches.
WHEN: Spring.
TIP: If killed to the ground after a cold winter, will resprout from the roots. Some species are evergreen.

Spicebush

LONICERA

Bush honeysuckles

GOAL: Control size and shape.
HOW TO PRUNE: When overgrown, prune one-third of the stems to the ground yearly.
WHEN: Early spring for major pruning; otherwise, anytime.

MAGNOLIA

Magnolias

GOAL: Control height and spread and remove poorly placed branches.
HOW TO PRUNE: Train to a framework when young, then little pruning is necessary. Cut off spent blooms rather than pinching. Thin excessive interior growth on star magnolia (M. *stellata*). Flowers on previous season's growth.
WHEN: Prune after flowering.
TIP: Magnolia bleeds in spring.

MYRICA PENSYLVANICA

Northern bayberry

GOAL: Control shape and remove suckers.
HOW TO PRUNE: Usually, little pruning is needed. Head back lightly to encourage compact form, if desired. Remove suckers that spoil the shape.
WHEN: Late winter or early spring.
TIP: Northern bayberry may also be semievergreen. May be cut back hard to renovate, if necessary.

ORNAMENTAL GRASSES

GOAL: Remove brown stems from the previous year before new growth starts.
HOW TO PRUNE: Cut back foliage of warm-season grasses (those that grow vigorously in warm months) to the ground once a year. Trim foliage of cool-season grasses (those that grow vigorously in cool months) by two-thirds. Use a weed whip, string trimmer, or chain saw to cut the clumps.
WHEN: Just before new growth starts. In mild-winter regions, cut warm-season grasses back in late fall.
TIP: In mild climates, you may not have to cut back cool-season grasses until they begin to look bad. Dormant foliage can be a fire hazard in some parts of the country.

PHILADELPHUS CORONARIUS

Mockorange

GOAL: Encourage new growth and vigorous flowering.
HOW TO PRUNE: Remove one-fourth of old stems each year. To renovate, cut stems back to base.
WHEN: Right after flowering. Renovation: early spring.
TIP: Flowers bloom on previous season's growth.

Mockorange

POTENTILLA FRUITICOSA

Bush cinquefoil

GOAL: To keep the shrub looking neat and to encourage flowering.
HOW TO PRUNE: Remove a third of old stems each year. Flowers on current growth.
WHEN: Spring. Trim anytime.

Bush cinquefoil

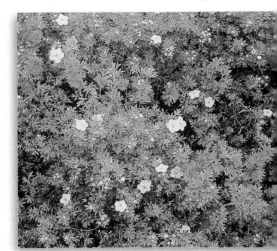

ENCYCLOPEDIA OF SHRUBS
continued

**Purple-leaf
sand cherry**

PRUNUS

Purple-leaf sand cherry, flowering almond, flowering apricot

GOAL: Stimulate new growth and remove crowded stems. Encourage abundant flowers.
HOW TO PRUNE: Cut one-third of the old stems of purple-leaf sand cherry (P. × cistena) back to the ground yearly. Prune one-fourth of oldest stems to 1 to 12 inches tall and head back stems that have finished blooming on flowering almond (P. glandulosa) and apricot (P. mume).
WHEN: Immediately after flowering.

PUNICA GRANATUM

Pomegranate

GOAL: Train as a tree or shrub and control height.
HOW TO PRUNE: As an ornamental shrub, train to multiple trunks. To train as a tree, pick out a central stem and remove side shoots. Remove unwanted suckers and thin lightly each year.
WHEN: Early spring.

RHODODENDRON

Deciduous species and cultivars

GOAL: Control size and encourage flowering. Remove dead wood and spent flowers as part of regular pruning.
HOW TO PRUNE: Thin to decrease size and remove suckers. Pinch new shoots to encourage branching. Remove twiggy growth. On leggy plants, cut one-fourth of oldest stems back to base annually for four years. Remove faded flowers. Rhododendron will tolerate heavy pruning, although it's usually not necessary.
WHEN: After flowering in spring. Pinch in late spring through midsummer.

RHUS TYPHINA

Staghorn sumac

GOAL: Control height, width, and spread. Keep suckers under control.
HOW TO PRUNE: Remove dead or crossing branches and unnecessary suckers. Keep size in bounds by cutting one-fourth to one-third of stems back to the ground each year.
WHEN: Early spring.
TIP: Staghorn forms suckering clumps if not controlled. Dig up the clumps and replant them elsewhere, give them to a friend, or discard them.

ROSA

Roses

GOAL: Extensive pruning to promote abundant flowering.
HOW TO PRUNE: Roses may be pruned lightly, moderately, or hard, depending on winter damage and the wishes of the grower. The usual practice with hybrid teas is to remove one-third to one-half of the previous year's growth. First remove dead canes to the crown, then cut off winter-damaged sections of canes below brown wood. Remove suckers. For more information on pruning roses, see pages 38 and 39.
WHEN: In late dormant season for most types of roses; after flowering for ramblers.

SPIRAEA

Spirea, bridal wreath

GOAL: Maintain natural shape (which varies from low and mounded to tall and arching, depending on species) and vigorous growth. Enhance flowering.
HOW TO PRUNE: Thin stems that have flowered. Rejuvenate overgrown shrubs by cutting one-third of old canes to the ground annually for three years.
WHEN: Early spring for species whose flowers are formed on current season's growth, such as Japanese, Japanese white, billiard, and crispleaf. After flowering for species whose blooms are on previous year's growth, such as vanhoutte spirea.

Stephanandra

STEPHANANDRA

GOAL: Maintain natural arching habit.
HOW TO PRUNE: Prune just enough to maintain shape. On overgrown plants, cut one-fourth of old stems back to base each year until renewed.
WHEN: After flowering.
TIP: The ends of arching stems that touch the ground will root.

SYMPLOCOS PANICULATA

Sapphireberry

GOAL: Encourage dense growth and abundant berries.
HOW TO PRUNE: Little pruning needed. Shorten too-long stems.
WHEN: Anytime.

SYRINGA VULGARIS

Lilac

GOAL: Encourage flowering along length of branch, not just tips; retain compact shape yet allow enough air flow through leaves to discourage mildew. Remove flowers.
HOW TO PRUNE: Remove spent blooms. Cut one-fourth of old canes to the ground. Remove suckers.
WHEN: After flowering.

TAMARIX

Tamarisk

GOAL: Control size and shape and encourage flowering.
HOW TO PRUNE: Remove weak growth on spring-flowering species and thin stems that have flowered. Cut summer-flowering species to the ground.
WHEN: Spring-flowering species, after blooms fade. Summer-flowering species, early spring.
TIP: May require occasional root pruning. Some species are evergreen.

VIBURNUM

Cranberrybush, Japanese snowball

GOAL: To maintain natural form and encourage abundant spring flowering.
HOW TO PRUNE: Little needed. Pinch off vertical water sprouts on doublefile viburnum (V. *plicatum tomentosum*). If overgrown, cut back one-fourth of old stems to ground yearly for four years. To train as a single- or multiple-trunk tree, choose the most likely stems when young and thin side shoots until the trunk reaches the desired height.
WHEN: After flowering.

Viburnum

WEIGELA

Weigela

GOAL: Encourage flowers and control size.
HOW TO PRUNE: Cut out winter-damaged stems. Remove one-third of remaining canes to base. Prune stems that have flowered to a strong bud. Head back wayward stems. Flowers on one-year-old wood.
WHEN: After flowering.

ENCYCLOPEDIA OF EVERGREEN AND DECIDUOUS VINES

Kolomikta vine

ACTINIDIA

Kolomikta vine, bower actinidia, tara vine

GOAL: Some species, such as bower vine (*A. arguta*), grow rampantly, so prune to control size. For less vigorous species, such as kolomikta (*A. kolomikta*), prune to encourage growth of new shoots.
HOW TO PRUNE: Prune established vines by one-third yearly; remove weak growth. Thin to control growth, head to promote growth.
WHEN: Late winter or early spring.
TIP: Blooms on old growth.

AKEBIA QUINATA

Five-leaf akebia

GOAL: Grows vigorously, up to 15 feet in one year. Prune to control size and shape of vine.
HOW TO PRUNE: In warm climates, cut vine to ground yearly. In cold climates, thin as necessary to keep plant in bounds; to rejuvenate, cut it to the ground.
WHEN: Warm climates, late winter. Cold climates, after flowering.
TIP: Five-leaf akebia can quickly get out of control in warm-winter climates.

ALLAMANDA CATHARTICA

Allamand

GOAL: Encourage dense growth and keep the plant looking neat.
HOW TO PRUNE: Pinch tips of new growth to encourage branching and develop bushy growth. Cut back all stems of mature vines to about 3 inches, if needed.
WHEN: Pinch in late spring or early summer. Prune the vine in spring before new growth starts.

Allamand

AMPELOPSIS BREVIPEDUNCULATA

Porcelain vine

GOAL: Grows rampantly; prune to keep vine in bounds and encourage fruit set.
HOW TO PRUNE: Shorten stems each year. Cut back to ground to renovate. Remove suckers.
WHEN: Late winter.
TIP: Vigorous grower that blooms and sets fruit on current season's growth.

ANTIGONON LEPTOPUS

Coral vine

GOAL: Control growth, avoid dense tangles, and keep vine in bounds.
HOW TO PRUNE: Cut back to within a foot of the ground.
WHEN: Late fall each year.

ARISTOLOCHIA DURIOR

Dutchman's pipe

GOAL: To keep growth in check and promote flowering.
HOW TO PRUNE: Remove all weak growth. Thin stems that have flowered. Pinch twice during the growing season to encourage branching. If overgrown, cut plant back to a foot tall.
WHEN: Late winter.
TIP: Dutchman's pipe flowers on previous season's growth.

BIGNONIA CAPREOLATA

Cross vine

GOAL: Control size of this vigorous evergreen vine while promoting new growth for blooms.
HOW TO PRUNE: Remove weak growth annually and shorten previous season's growth by two-thirds.
WHEN: Early spring.
TIP: Blooms on current season's growth.

BOUGAINVILLEA

GOAL: Keep in bounds and encourage abundant flower production.
HOW TO PRUNE: Remove dead material and shape the vine. Prune previous year's growth to three buds. If bougainvillea has become too crowded, remove one-fourth of old stems. Cut off suckers at the base of mature vines.
WHEN: Late winter or early spring, after flowering.
TIP: For the first two years after planting, tie the strongest shoots to the support in an evenly spaced fan shape; remove weak shoots. Blooms on current season's growth.

CAMPSIS RADICANS

Trumpet creeper

GOAL: Keep rampant growth in check.
HOW TO PRUNE: Remove all suckers and pinch growing tips to encourage the vine to branch. Trim to control size.
WHEN: Late winter or early spring. Blooms on current season's wood.

CELASTRUS SCANDENS

Bittersweet

GOAL: Keep these aggressive vines in bounds.
HOW TO PRUNE: Prune hard yearly for best flowering and to control size. Dig up suckers at base and remove branches that fruited the previous year. If vine is overgrown, cut entire plant back to 6 to 12 inches high.
WHEN: Early spring.

Bittersweet

Clematis viticella

CLEMATIS

GOAL: Eliminate tangles, increase flowering, and remove unproductive wood.
GROUP A: Blooms in late spring to summer on last season's growth. (Example: *C. armandii, C. montana, C. macropetala, C. alpina, C. afoliata, C. cirrhosa, C. indivisa, C. vitalba.*)
HOW TO PRUNE: Prune lightly to keep the vine in shape. Remove weak or damaged growth back to a healthy bud. Can be cut to the ground, but thick stems may not resprout.
WHEN: Right after flowering.
GROUP B: Blooms in early summer on the previous year's growth and later has a light flush of blooms on the current season's growth. (Example: 'Nelly Moser', 'Barbara Jackman', 'Belle of Woking', 'King Edward VIII', 'H.F. Young', 'Hagley Hybrid', and all double-flowered varieties.)
HOW TO PRUNE: Three choices:
■ Prune once every three years by cutting the vine back to 1 foot tall in early spring.
■ Or, prune half of the vine hard one year before growth begins and the other half the next year.
■ Or, remove dead and weak growth during early spring, then wait until after flowering to shorten the stems that bloomed.
WHEN: Late winter, before growth, or lightly in early spring and again after first blooms fade.
GROUP C: Flowers late in the season on new growth. (Example: *C. × jackmanii, C. flammula, C. orientalis,* and *C. viticella.*)
HOW TO PRUNE: Cut back yearly to a pair of buds 12 inches from ground level. Remove stems killed by frost.
WHEN: Early spring, with first signs of growth.
TIP: All clematis have a pair of buds, one on each side of a stem, so a straight cut will produce new growth on both sides.

ENCYCLOPEDIA OF EVERGREEN AND DECIDUOUS VINES
continued

EUONYMUS FORTUNEI

Wintercreeper

GOAL: Direct the vine's growth and keep it in check. Train as a spreading or climbing vine or shrub.
HOW TO PRUNE: Remove dead material and cut back stems as needed. Rejuvenate by cutting to the ground.
WHEN: Late dormant season or early in spring.
TIP: If training wintercreeper to a wall or fence, pinch tips of young shoots to encourage branching.

FICUS PUMILA

Creeping fig

GOAL: Direct growth, keep vine in a juvenile state with small leaves, and prevent vine from being intrusive in favorable climates.
HOW TO PRUNE: Soon after planting, cut the vine back almost to the ground. This will encourage new stems to develop. Thin the vine by removing weak growth and up to one-fourth of old branches. Pinch tips of branches during summer to encourage bushiness. Maintain regular pruning.
WHEN: Early spring.
TIP: May need harder pruning in hot climates to keep under control.

GELSEMIUM SEMPERVIRENS

Carolina jessamine, yellow jessamine, evening trumpet flower, or Carolina jasmine

GOAL: Promote bushy growth and abundant flowering. Train as a vine or as an effective ground cover.
HOW TO PRUNE: Remove weak or crowded growth to shape vine. Pinch young vines to encourage a bushy habit. When overgrown, cut one-third of the oldest stems to the ground.
WHEN: Prune after blooming.
TIP: Carolina jessamine blooms on previous season's wood.

HEDERA HELIX

English ivy

GOAL: Direct growth and keep vine in bounds and in vigorous juvenile state with small leaves. Train as a climbing vine or ground cover.
HOW TO PRUNE: Trim stems as needed to control size. When grown as a ground cover, it may be mowed with the blade set high or trimmed with hedge shears. To renovate overgrown ivy, trim all stems back to 3 feet in length, cutting to within ¼ inch of a bud.
WHEN: Early spring.

Creeping fig

English ivy

HUMULUS LUPULUS

Hops

GOAL: Remove winter-killed shoots and increase fruit production.
HOW TO PRUNE: Cut to ground.
WHEN: Winter or early spring.
TIP: Take care when training stems to a sturdy trellis in summer. Young shoots break easily.

HYDRANGEA ANOMALA

Climbing hydrangea

GOAL: Encourage abundant growth and flowers and control size.
HOW TO PRUNE: Shorten shoots that have grown too long. Cut overgrown vines back by one-third over three years. Can be cut back severely, if necessary, to limit spread and encourage growth of new wood. But vine won't bloom again for several years afterward.
WHEN: Late winter or early spring.
TIP: Climbing hydrangea takes about three years to become established. After that, it grows rapidly. It blooms on the current season's wood.

Climbing hydrangea

IPOMOEA

Moonflower, sweet potato vine, and cardinal climber

GOAL: Promote flowers and control congested growth.
HOW TO PRUNE: Cut perennial species to the ground each year.
WHEN: Late winter.

Common hop

JASMINUM

Winter jasmine, common white jasmine, showy jasmine

GOAL: Control rapid growth as well as promote new growth and flower production.
HOW TO PRUNE: Cut out weak shoots and overcrowded growth. May remove up to one-third of the vine each year to keep it in bounds.
WHEN: Right after flowering.
TIP: Blooms on previous summer's shoots. If not pruned annually, jasmine develops dead material beneath its new stems. Arching stems that touch the ground will root. Tie stems to a support to prevent this from happening.

KADSURA JAPONICA

Scarlet kadsura

GOAL: Control size and shape of vine.
HOW TO PRUNE: Thin and shape to keep vine in bounds. Prune top growth so that it doesn't shade the lower part of vine.
WHEN: Late winter or early spring.
TIP: Cut back one old branch of scarlet kadsura mature vines to the ground every other year.

LATHYRUS

Sweetpeas and beach pea

GOAL: Remove winter dieback and encourage new growth.
HOW TO PRUNE: In cold-winter climates, cut vines to the ground yearly. In warm-winter areas, cut out weak, dead, or damaged growth.
WHEN: In cold climates, prune in early spring. In warm climates, after flowering.

ENCYCLOPEDIA OF EVERGREEN AND DECIDUOUS VINES
continued

LONICERA

Japanese, goldflame, trumpet honeysuckles, and woodbine

GOAL: Some species are rampant, aggressive, and invasive. Prune to keep in bounds.
HOW TO PRUNE: Japanese honeysuckle (*L. japonica*): Remove suckers and prune hard annually because flowers are borne on the current season's growth. Head other loniceras back by one-fourth to maintain size and shape. To renovate mature plants, cut one-fourth of the old stems to the ground level each year for four years.
WHEN: Prune Japanese honeysuckle anytime; renovate in late winter. Prune others after flowering.
TIP: Japanese honeysuckle is such a rampant grower that it can quickly become a weed. Its stems will root wherever they touch the ground. Vines strangle trees and shrubs in their path and form a tangle of growth.

MANDEVILLA

Chilean jasmine, mandevilla

GOAL: Encourage new growth and avoid congested old growth.
HOW TO PRUNE: Remove weak and crowded stems and cut back tips of stems to keep plant in bounds and encourage dense growth. Cut Chilean jasmine to the ground to renovate, if needed.
WHEN: Prune hybrid mandevilla after flowering. Prune others in late winter or early spring. Remove spent blooms.

MUEHLENBECKIA COMPLEXA

Wire plant

GOAL: To maintain its "tracery" pattern of growth yet keep growth in check.
HOW TO PRUNE: Prune only enough to keep the plant in bounds. Aggressive pruning destroys the branching habit (the "tracery").
WHEN: Early spring.

Mandevilla

PARTHENOCISSUS

Virginia creeper, Boston ivy, and silver vein creeper

GOAL: Direct growth and keep in bounds.
HOW TO PRUNE: Cut off stems that are growing out of bounds. To renovate, cut the vine to the ground.
WHEN: Early spring before growth starts. Light pruning or shaping is okay during the growing season.
TIP: When a holdfast comes loose, remove the stem because it can't reattach itself.

PASSIFLORA

Blue passion flower and wild passion flower

GOAL: Evergreen and deciduous vines that run rampantly. Prune to keep growth in check.
HOW TO PRUNE: Remove weak, overgrown, and dead stems. Head and thin vine enough to keep in bounds. If passion flower isn't blooming much or has become overgrown, cut it back to the ground to renovate.
WHEN: Spring.

Passion flower

POLYGONUM AUBERTII

Silver lace vine

GOAL: A vigorous, invasive vine. Prune to keep in bounds and stimulate flower production.
HOW TO PRUNE: Cut all stems back by one-third yearly. Can renovate by cutting the vine to a foot tall.
WHEN: In early spring, before new growth begins. Blooms on new growth.
TIP: Hard pruning encourages new growth and many flowers.

SCHIZOPHRAGMA HYDRANGEOIDES

Hydrangea vine

GOAL: Promote new growth and flowers yet keep vine in bounds.
HOW TO PRUNE: Shorten shoots and thin overly vigorous growth.
WHEN: Early spring before new growth starts.
TIP: Blooms on new growth.

Hydrangea vine

SOLANUM

Potato vine

GOAL: To promote new growth yet keep vine in bounds.
HOW TO PRUNE: Pinch tips of new growth to encourage branching. Trim stems to three or four vigorous buds to control size. Spread renovation over three years rather than pruning hard at one time.
WHEN: Early spring before plant begins growing.
TIP: Blooms on new growth.

STAUNTONIA HEXAPHYLLA

Stauntonia

GOAL: To control size and encourage flowering.
HOW TO PRUNE: Cut vine to 12 inches high to promote new growth on which vines bloom.
WHEN: Early spring before growth starts.

TRACHELOSPERMUM JASMINOIDES

Star jasmine

GOAL: Promote flowering.
HOW TO PRUNE: Needs little pruning. Flowers grow on spurs like wisteria. Blooms on previous year's growth.
WHEN: Early spring before growth is evident.
TIP: If blooming decreases, cut back by half. Star jasmine's habit is naturally dense.

VITIS COIGNETIAE

Crimson glory vine

GOAL: Keep growth in bounds and stimulate blooming.
HOW TO PRUNE: Head back vine at planting time to induce growth of lateral branches. As vines mature, cut them back to healthy buds to maintain size and shape. Flowers grow on spurs. Shorten last year's growth and side shoots to two to three buds in winter. Renovate by pruning to 1 foot tall.
WHEN: Midwinter before sap rises.

WISTERIA

GOAL: Keep growth in check and stimulate flower production.
HOW AND WHEN TO PRUNE: Flowers on spurs, like grapes. Let a young vine grow unpruned until it has reached the desired size. In winter thin all new growth to the second bud. In spring remove all leafless shoots. Prune side branches to two or three buds, leaving the spurs. In summer remove leafless shoots and shorten laterals by half. Support main branches well because they become thick and heavy as the vine branches during the year. Remove suckers on grafted varieties.
TIP: For first three years, train wisteria to a framework with one trunk and several evenly spaced main stems. Cutting back severely each year causes excessive foliage growth at the expense of flowers. Root pruning curbs overly vigorous shoot growth and encourages flowering. Grows on flower spurs. Blooms on mature wood.

Wisteria

PRUNING EVERGREEN TREES AND SHRUBS

The evergreens shown here are needled rather than broadleaf. With leaves reduced to needles, plants better resist cold weather and drying winds.

Just as deciduous trees and shrubs grow in various shapes dictated by their branching patterns, so do evergreens. They may be rounded, spreading, conical, upright, oval, weeping, or irregular. One of the main goals in pruning evergreen shrubs and trees is to preserve the plants' natural form while limiting their size.

Evergreens are divided into two distinct groups: needled and broadleaf. The way you prune depends on which group the plant belongs to.

NEEDLED EVERGREENS

Also called conifers, needled evergreens have narrow, needlelike leaves. With these minimized leaves, the plants are able to resist low temperatures and drying winds. Needled evergreens can be further divided into two more groups: those that grow from terminal buds and those with random buds on their stems. (There are also deciduous needled conifers—dawn redwood, larch, golden larch, and bald cypress—which are discussed in the chapter on deciduous trees.)

TERMINAL BUDS: Most evergreens send out one flush of growth each spring, which matures by midsummer. New buds then develop but remain dormant until the next year. Many needled evergreens, including pines, firs, cedars, and spruces, grow only from terminal buds on the end of the branches. Usually, several buds are at the terminals, producing a whorled branching pattern. The resulting new growth is called a candle because it starts out pressed into a narrow, cylindrical shape. Candles are lighter green than older growth and are more flexible.

Needled evergreens have few if any latent buds, and the ones they do have remain active for only a few years. Also, they rarely form adventitious buds. So if cuts are made into older, leafless areas, these terminal-bud evergreens don't regrow. Some, such as pine, won't regrow unless buds are actually visible, even if the stem has foliage.

Because the main reason for pruning candled trees or shrubs is to keep the plants bushy, the best way to prune is to pinch half of the candle before it expands completely.

RANDOM BUDS: Evergreens with random buds are often called narrowleaf because they have scalelike needles compressed against their stem, such as arborvitae, juniper, cypress, and cedar. In the random branching pattern, new branches may grow anywhere along the trunk and old stems, and plants

Broadleaf evergreens, such as camellias, have green foliage year-round. But unlike needled evergreens, this group produces flowers.

grow in spurts throughout spring and summer. Because of that, most tolerate severe pruning. However, arborvitae will not regrow if pruned into wood without visible buds. Yews and junipers will resprout from old wood only if it still has foliage.

Prune random-bud evergreens by thinning wayward growth. To keep them from growing too large, slightly shorten their branches in late winter.

BROADLEAF EVERGREENS

Broadleaf evergreens have wide leaves like those of deciduous plants. Popular broadleaf evergreens include azalea, boxwood, camellia, holly, mahonia, mountain laurel, southern magnolia, rhododendron, and Japanese pieris. In cold climates, broadleaf evergreens may be semievergreen or even deciduous.

Some broadleaf evergreens, such as rhododendrons, grow just from the terminal, with leaf buds sprouting below the flower buds. Dormant buds develop at the stem tips in midsummer for the next spring's growth. Many other broadleaf evergreens, including azaleas, pyracantha, and holly, develop latent or adventitious buds. These you can rejuvenate by cutting into old wood.

TIPS

For most evergreens, pruning at a precise time of year is not important. But if you want to keep plants growing slowly and within bounds, prune them just after new growth stops, usually late spring or early summer.

If pruned while new growth is still soft, some evergreens develop new buds. No new buds will form after the new growth has hardened. The pruned tips may then become dead twigs.

Junipers, arborvitae, cypress, and false cypress can be pruned safely at any time, but it is best to prune them before or during new growth. Avoid pruning in late summer.

Pines pruned during a dry summer or in any kind of summer in southern areas are prone to attack by bark beetles. Sometimes they attack in such numbers as to kill the tree.

EVERGREENS YOU CAN CUT BACK HARD

Azalea	Japanese cedar
Pyracantha	China fir
Rhododendron	Redwood
Chinese plum yew	Yew

Blue spruce, a pyramidal evergreen, looks most attractive in its natural form, with its wide branches growing to the ground.

EVERGREEN GROWTH PATTERNS

Pyramidal

Columnar

Irregular

Rounded

Weeping

Prostrate

Conical

PRUNING NEEDLED EVERGREEN SHRUBS

Use hedge trimmers to shear needled evergreen hedges into formal shapes.

Needled evergreen shrubs are popular because they make wonderful foundation plants. Available in a wide variety of shapes, colors, and sizes, needled evergreen shrubs will be a dependable element in your landscape's design, year in and year out.

To keep them looking their best, they must be pruned correctly. Many of these plants—especially yew, juniper, arborvitae, and false cypress—can quickly get out of hand if not trained correctly. And they will require annual pruning to stay in check.

Alternatives to consider when selecting needled evergreen shrubs are dwarf or slow-growing varieties. Although they cost more initially because they are slow to grow to a marketable size, planting them instead of standard-size shrubs will greatly reduce your maintenance time in the long run.

To thin an informal needled shrub, reach into the interior and cut a branch back to its parent branch.

TECHNIQUES

SHEARING: To create a formal appearance for evergreen shrubs, shearing with hedge shears or trimmers is the easiest technique. Evergreen shrubs with random buds seem to respond the best to shearing.

As with deciduous plants, shearing induces denser growth on the outside edge of the shrub and causes the plant to grow larger (see illustration, top right). For that reason, shearing is a high-maintenance task, which you may want to limit to use on hedges. Once you begin shearing a needled evergreen shrub, it will continue to need regular trimming forever after.

The time to shear is in winter or early spring so that the new growth will hide the cuts. Then lightly shear once again in early to midsummer if new growth warrants it. Don't wait too long to shear. Shearing an evergreen shrub in late summer or in fall leads to soft new growth that may be killed by cold weather. The snipped leaves will be unsightly all winter as well.

THINNING: This is the best method to use with needled evergreen shrubs. If done regularly, it effectively controls their size. Unlike shearing, it doesn't stimulate excessive growth.

Use loppers or hand pruners to thin evergreen shrubs in late winter or early spring, when plants are dormant. Or, perform touch-up pruning in late spring just after a spurt of growth. Selectively remove branches to maintain the natural shape while opening the shrub to more light. Cut back to a main branch or to the trunk, leaving no stubs. Remember to avoid cutting into old growth, which, on most needled evergreen shrubs, won't resprout. You can remove up to one quarter of the branches by thinning each year.

If quite a bit of thinning is needed, start at the top of the shrub and work downward, pruning on alternate sides of the shrub as you go. Prune more lightly as you progress down. This will help preserve the shrub's natural shape. Because upper branches receive the most sun, they will grow the fastest and need more aggressive pruning than lower branches.

PINCHING: You can encourage denser growth on needled evergreen shrubs that develop candles by pinching the new growth in half during late spring to early summer as the candle begins to expand. It's important to get the timing right because pines, such as mugo, won't form new buds near cuts unless they're pruned while they're actively growing.

PRUNING SYMMETRICAL, NEEDLED EVERGREEN SHRUBS

Sometimes owners must give Mother Nature a hand in maintaining needled evergreen shrubs that grow in symmetrical pyramidal

Shearing a needled evergreen for a formal look removes many growing points at once. Latent buds break dormancy, resulting in denser growth on the exterior of the plant.

forms. Prune wayward branches by thinning them back to an inward-growing side branch, which will form a new stem that should grow upward and outward toward the light.

SHINGLE CUTS: Illustration A at right shows you how to taper an upright shrub so that it remains narrow at the top and wider at the bottom. Use thinning cuts, not shearing. Trimming the upper branches so they are the shortest exposes the lower branches to the sun and helps keep them full and healthy.

With one hand, lift up the branch to be pruned. Holding the pruning shears in the other hand, reach beneath the branch into the shrub. Cut the branch at the point where it meets a side branch or the parent stem. With this "shingle cut" method, longer, overhanging branches camouflage the cut ends so the shrub maintains its natural appearance.

You can use a similar technique to maintain the natural shingled shape of a spreading needled evergreen (see illustration B, at right). Thinning in this manner maintains shapeliness and promotes dense, compact growth, keeping the plant handsome and in bounds for years to come.

PROSTRATE JUNIPERS

When junipers grown as ground covers reach the edge of the sidewalk or curb, they must be cut back. What often happens is that owners whack off the branches that are too long, leaving ugly, bare stems.

Instead of shearing or lopping off the ends of the stems, use hand pruners to thin stems from underneath, much like the shingle cut. Doing this will give them a more attractive, natural appearance, and it doesn't promote

excessive growth that will soon need trimming again.

PRUNING NEW SHRUBS

At many nurseries, young needled evergreens are sheared to encourage bushiness or fullness. True, this increases fullness on the outside of the plant; however, it doesn't encourage growth of interior branches.

For the first two years after bringing home and planting new needled evergreen shrubs, thin them to loosen the tight growth and allow light and air into the interior. By the third year, the shrub should have a normal appearance.

A

B

A: Prune upright yews using thinning cuts hidden beneath overhanging foliage. Taper the shape of the shrub from top to bottom.

B: For a spreading yew, prune with thinning cuts to emphasize the shingled look of the branches.

PRUNING BROADLEAF EVERGREEN SHRUBS

Andromeda is a broadleaf evergreen that requires little pruning. Just remove faded blooms after flowering and thin the plant if it becomes leggy.

Broadleaf evergreen shrubs such as pyracantha, holly, and boxwood are pruned more like deciduous shrubs rather than needled evergreens. They rarely need as frequent pruning as deciduous shrubs, though. In fact, slow-growing broadleaf evergreens may never need to be pruned.

Because many broadleaf evergreen shrubs flower or produce berries, the time that they bloom or form fruit is a consideration when pruning them. The best time to prune blooming broadleaf evergreens is immediately after flowering, while late winter or early spring is ideal for berried bushes. However, pruning while the shrub is flowering lets you see how much you are removing so you can have both: berries in fall and flowers the next year. Shrubs without flowers or berries should be pruned in late winter or early spring.

Many of the basic duties for pruning broadleaf evergreen shrubs are the same as for other shrub pruning. First remove all diseased, dead, or damaged areas, cutting back to healthy buds on the branch or to the main trunk. Thin selected branches to control size and reduce height, keeping in mind the natural form of the shrub.

Using hedge shears on broadleaf evergreen shrubs is not recommended because their leaves are so large. Shearing mutilates the foliage, and the shrubs are left looking awful. The best tools for pruning broadleaved shrubs are hand pruners and loppers (and a pruning saw for old specimens). However, you may shear small-leafed evergreens, such as boxwood or Japanese holly, particularly when they are used in a hedge.

REJUVENATING BROADLEAF EVERGREENS

If you've inherited a broadleaf evergreen shrub that hasn't previously been thinned to control height and width, you may have to resort to a three- or four-year renovation. Cut one-third to one-fourth of the oldest stems to the ground each year in early spring. This encourages new growth and helps side shoots develop.

An easy way to rejuvenate hollies and other vigorous growers in mild-winter climates is to cut them back to 3 or 4 inches tall in early spring and let them grow back. Not all will, but if the shrub was so overgrown that it would have had to be replaced anyway, this method is certainly worth trying.

Another method that works well on a large, neglected holly is called "hat-racking." Cut back the top branches to short stubs. Then, working downward, increase the length of the pruned branches to shape the plant into a pyramid. The plant will look unsightly after pruning, but, because new growth readily sprouts from latent buds, the holly will regain its natural shape in a couple of years.

TIPS FOR RHODODENDRONS

Once flowers have faded, remove them so they don't sap the energy the plant normally

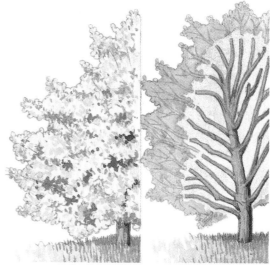

Overgrown broadleaf shrubs crowd walkways and neighboring plants. Keep them in bounds by thinning major limbs to side branches.

The best way to prune broadleaf shrubs is to selectively thin wayward growth, keeping in mind the natural shape of the shrub.

devotes to growing leaves and buds. (See illustration for the best way to deadhead rhododendrons.) Deadheading also prevents the shrubs from blooming heavily in alternate years. If you can't reach all the brown blossoms because the rhododendron is too tall, knock them off with a strong blast of water from a hose.

Don't let dead branches accumulate inside the plant. Trim them off to the first live rosette of leaves or remove the whole branch. Also remove suckers on older, grafted rhododendrons. These divert energy from the main plant and have different flowers.

If a rhododendron becomes leggy, with most of its leaves at the ends of the branches, prune it in early spring by cutting back to 4 to 5 inches above a fork in the main stem. A dormant bud in that area will begin growing. When the interior of a rhododendron becomes crowded, thin the shrub over several years to let light inside.

TIPS FOR CAMELLIAS

You can do minor maintenance and shaping on camellias at anytime, but wait until after blooms fade to do major pruning. Avoid heading back camellias because that often leads to long, lanky new growth.

Prune a camellia by cutting just above the slightly thickened bud scale scar (see page 8), which signals where one year's growth ends and another begins. This forces three or four dormant buds into growth, helping to ensure a bushier shrub. All camellias except *Camellia reticulata* can tolerate heavy pruning when necessary.

To avoid dropped buds and ensure larger flowers on Japanese camellia (*C. japonica*), disbud or remove some of the excess buds. Note that camellia flower buds are plump; leaf buds are slender.

To encourage branching on rhododendrons, wait until new growth is 4 inches long, then pinch off about 1 inch of stem just above a set of leaves (left).

To deadhead a rhododendron, remove faded flowers by bending them and snapping off gently (right).

TIPS FOR EVERGREEN AZALEAS

After azaleas bloom, pinch the tips to encourage bushier growth. Shearing an azalea during summer interferes with bud formation as well as reduces the crop of flowers. It also disturbs the natural shape of the shrub.

To renovate an evergreen azalea, cut one-third of the older branches back to 6 to 12 inches high each year for three years. Some species will tolerate even harder pruning.

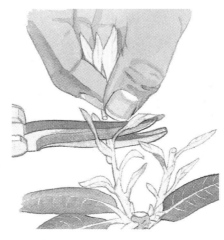

PRUNING EVERGREEN TREES

Japanese cedar, a needled evergreen, remains green even in the coldest regions of the United States.

Pruning a broadleaf evergreen tree such as southern magnolia is much the same as pruning a deciduous tree. Thin dense growth to let light into the tree's center, cut off competing leaders, and remove wayward branches that spoil the natural form. It's best to prune most broadleaf evergreens when they are young because large wounds close slowly.

TRAINING YOUNG EVERGREEN TREES

Broadleaved evergreens, needled evergreens, and many deciduous trees are similar in that a central leader is important to all. Pine, fir, hemlock, spruce, and other conifers usually develop a central leader naturally. If a leader is broken, a new one may develop from a bud nearest the damaged leader. Immediately cut off competing leaders if more than one develops. If a new leader doesn't develop, bend a side shoot near the broken leader upward and tie it to a wooden splint. Leave this in place until the leader can stay upright on its own, which may take as long as two years.

Some needled evergreen trees are sheared at the nursery to keep them neat. When they outgrow this shape in a year or two, don't shear them again. Let the tree grow for a year, then use selective thinning cuts to let in light. Selective pruning produces a less rigid outline and controls size better than shearing.

PINCHING OFF CANDLES

In many respects, needled evergreen trees are pruned like needled evergreen shrubs. To maintain compact size, pinch the top and side candles. Cut the candles with hand pruners at a 45-degree angle to minimize the possibility that a second leader will develop. It's important to pinch before the new candles harden. Some candles, such as those of white pines (*Pinus strobus*), harden quite early and must be pruned by early summer.

Pinching off half the new growth results in a bushier tree. If you would like to reduce the size of the tree, cut below the year-old growth into two-year-old wood.

Lower limbs sweeping the ground and a strong pyramidal shape defines the beauty of many evergreens. Removing their lower branches makes the trees look top heavy. The limbs won't grow back, and rarely will new branches grow to replace them. So think long and hard before cutting them off. Pines are an exception. Their lower limbs often die from being shaded by upper limbs. Because of their irregular habit, pines look okay after losing their lower limbs.

THINNING BRANCHES

Clear away dead needles and other debris in the center of the tree so you can see what you're doing. Then cleanly cut crowded shoots and branches growing in the wrong direction at their base. Don't prune into bare inner branches because these won't regrow.

Most conifers have a prominent branch collar (see page 23), so be sure to only cut to the collar and not into it. If you do, the wound might not close correctly.

SHEARING NEEDLED EVERGREENS

Have you ever noticed that when you shear a needled evergreen, the ends of the stems turn pinkish-brown? One way to avoid this is by shearing the tree when it's wet from dew or immediately after a rain. (Do this only with manual, gas- or battery-powered hedge shears; never use electric trimmers when the ground or plant is wet.)

When you shear, keep in mind the tree's natural shape. Although shearing "smooths the edges" of an evergreen tree, it shouldn't change its basic form. Let the top come to a point, which helps to prevent a heavy snowfall from weighing down the tree, and make sure to prune the lower branches so they stretch farther out than the upper ones and, thus, can intercept plenty of sunlight.

REJUVENATING EVERGREEN TREES

Overgrown evergreen trees, especially needled evergreens, are difficult to renovate because they cannot be cut back to old branches. They are best thinned while young to avoid becoming overgrown.

Broadleaf evergreen trees can be rejuvenated much the same as a deciduous tree, however, spread the renovation over three or four years rather than doing it all at once.

PATCHES OF DEAD NEEDLES

If you notice a section of brown needles in the tree or shrub, identify its cause so you can correct the situation. If the cause is a canker, gall rust, or other disease, prune the limb to the trunk. If it is needlecast or an insect, such as sawfly, treat the problem with the appropriate fungicide or insecticide.

If an evergreen's leader has broken, tie a stake to the tree's trunk. Select a side branch from the first whorl of branches below the lost leader and tie it to the stake. Within a few years, the stem will naturally grow as a central leader.

Identifying the problem may require the help of a county extension agent or professional arborist. Either should also be able to give you advice for treating the problem.

Cutting out the brown patch may reveal a gap or opening. Although new growth will eventually fill in the opening, in the meantime it can look unsightly if the tree is in a prominent location. You can improve the tree's appearance by tying a short wooden stake to the main branch near the gap. Then tie nearby shoots to the stake to fill in. Soon new growth will take over, and you can remove the stake.

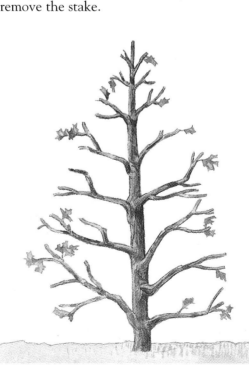

To whip an unruly holly into shape, "hat rack" it (left). Trim branches back to short stubs, increasing their length as you work down the shrub. This illustration has been stylized to show you the technique. When you attempt hat racking, don't take off excess foliage. Remove only the foliage on the branches you are shortening.

ENCYCLOPEDIA OF EVERGREEN TREES

White fir

ABIES

Firs

GOAL: Maintain strong central leader and symmetrical form.
TYPE: Terminal buds.
HOW TO PRUNE: Needs little pruning. Remove dead or broken branches and competing leaders. Lightly shear or laterally prune bottom branches if they spread too broadly. If leader is lost, train a neighboring branch to replace it.
WHEN: In spring before new growth begins.
TIP: Don't top the tree or cut beyond the foliage on a branch. Removing lower limbs destroys the beauty of this tree.

ACACIA

Bailey acacia or golden mimosa, and black acacia

GOAL: Promote broad spread, train as a single- or multi-trunked tree, and open center to light and air.
TYPE: Broadleaf.
HOW TO PRUNE: Remove branches that form narrow, V-shaped crotches. They are weak and can break. Remove suckers to maintain single trunk. Thin crown to open center. For multiple trunks, head back to encourage lower branches.
WHEN: Can prune anytime, but late spring is best for bailey or golden mimosa (*A. baileyana*). Prune after flowering to control size. Summer is recommended for black acacia (*A. melanoxylon*).
TIP: For a tree shape, remove lowest branches (cutting them back to the trunk). This tree can be pruned hard if necessary.

ARAUCARIA ARAUCANA

Monkey puzzle tree

GOAL: Maintain strong central leader.
TYPE: Random buds.
HOW TO PRUNE: Remove dead and dying branches and debris. Replace damaged or lost leader.
WHEN: While dormant.

Strawberry tree

ARBUTUS MENZIESII

Madrone or strawberry tree

GOAL: Maintain natural shape and remove dead material.
TYPE: Broadleaf.
HOW TO PRUNE: Needs little pruning except to train into a tree shape rather than as a shrub. You may want to gradually limb up trees or thin interior branches to expose the attractive exfoliating bark.
WHEN: Early spring.
TIP: Can cut back hard, if necessary.

BRACHYCHITON POPULNEUS

Bottle tree or flame tree

GOAL: Maintain strong central leader and natural shape.
TYPE: Broadleaf.
HOW TO PRUNE: Needs little pruning except for regular grooming and removal of dead wood. Gradually remove limbs below 10 feet, if desired.
WHEN: Dormant season.
TIP: Bottle tree has a natural central leader.

CALOCEDRUS DECURRENS

Incense cedar

GOAL: Maintain natural symmetrical shape.
TYPE: Random buds.
HOW TO PRUNE: Thin as needed to maintain shape. Don't remove lower limbs. Can be sheared into a hedge.
WHEN: Shearing: anytime. Other trimming: when dormant.
TIP: Natural shape is conical to pyramidal.

CASUARINA EQUISETIFOLIA

Beefwood

GOAL: Maintain strong form and remove dead material.
TYPE: Random buds.
HOW TO PRUNE: Train to a central leader with well-spaced scaffolding branches. Prune only to shape or to remove dead and broken branches. Beefwood may try to develop several trunks. Remove all but the best one.
WHEN: Anytime.

CEDRUS

Atlas cedar, deodar cedar, and cedar of Lebanon

GOAL: Maintain a strong central leader, remove dead wood and weak branches, and on deodar, maintain compactness.
TYPE: Terminal buds.
HOW TO PRUNE: Need little pruning if planted where they have room to grow. On atlas cedar (*C. atlantica*), thin out branches that mat together. Remove lower limbs to expose silvery bark, if desired. (However, trees are most beautiful when branched to the ground.) Remove dead branches on cedar of Lebanon (*C. libani*). Deodar cedar (*C. deodora*) tolerates shearing. To control its width, cut side branches back to half of their new growth.
WHEN: Perform major pruning in spring, while the tree is still dormant; thin as needed to control density. Exception: Prune deodar cedar in late spring.
TIP: Branches of young atlas cedars may appear to be too long and heavy. This corrects itself as the tree grows. The shape of a young cedar of Lebanon is pyramidal, but the tree spreads as it ages. Do not cut back beyond the needles on a branch because the tree will not develop new growth.

Incense cedar

Weeping atlas cedar

CEPHALOTAXUS FORTUNEI

Plum yew

GOAL: To maintain the tree's layered appearance.
TYPE: Random buds.
HOW TO PRUNE: Requires little pruning except occasional thinning to maintain horizontal branching pattern. Do not remove upright-growing limbs that bear tiers of horizontal branches. These are normal and help give the tree its shape.
WHEN: In spring before new growth begins.
TIP: One of the few evergreens you can prune hard (or beyond the foliage) because new growth will come from old wood.

ENCYCLOPEDIA OF EVERGREEN TREES
continued

Yellow false cypress

Japanese cedar

CHAMAECYPARIS

Lawson, yellow, and Japanese false cypresses

GOAL: Control height and width.
TYPE: Random buds.
HOW TO PRUNE: Pinch tips of branches to encourage new growth. Thin regularly for best appearance and to control height and width. Can shear lawson cypress (*C. lawsoniana*) as a large shrub, if desired. On Japanese false cypress (*C. pisifera*), remove buildup of dead material in interior of the tree. Train lawson cypress to a central leader when tree is young.
WHEN: Spring before new growth begins. Perform touch-up pruning as necessary.
TIP: Drooping lower branches can root if touching the ground. Do not cut back into bare branches when pruning.

CINNAMOMUM CAMPHORA

Camphor tree

GOAL: Maintain a strong central leader and keep branches limbed up to about 6 feet off the ground.
TYPE: Broadleaf.
HOW TO PRUNE: Remove dead or damaged branches. On young trees, direct branches outward instead of upward to encourage a graceful form when the tree matures.
WHEN: Major pruning in early spring while the tree is still dormant. Otherwise, anytime as necessary.

CLETHRA ARBOREA

Sweet alder

GOAL: Maintain the tree's natural shape.
HOW TO PRUNE: Needs little pruning. Remove dead or broken branches as needed.
TYPE: Broadleaf.
WHEN: Spring.
TIP: If the tree freezes to the ground, select the strongest shoot that develops the next summer to train as the tree's central leader. Sometimes grown as a large shrub.

CRYPTOMERIA JAPONICA

Japanese cedar

GOAL: Maintain natural form by removing limbs growing out of bounds.
TYPE: Terminal buds.
HOW TO PRUNE: Needs little pruning except to shape. Pinch tips for dense growth.
WHEN: Spring or summer. Do major pruning when trees are dormant.
TIP: Gardeners often prune 'Elagans' Japanese cedar into oriental shapes. If necessary, stake its trunk, which may be weak.

CUNNINGHAMIA LANCEOLATA

China fir

GOAL: Maintain a central leader with horizontal scaffolding branches. Preserve whorled branching pattern for an exotic look.
TYPE: Terminal buds.
HOW TO PRUNE: Remove suckers at base and prune dead limbs back to trunk.
WHEN: Spring and summer.
TIP: Will tolerate heavy pruning, although it is rarely necessary. This tree often sheds its branches; remove them as necessary.

CUPRESSUS

Cypresses

GOAL: Encourage and maintain a single central leader.
TYPE: Random buds.
HOW TO PRUNE: Rarely need pruning except to remove dead branches and perform regular grooming. The natural form of Monterey cypress (*C. macrocarpa*) is best, but it can be sheared.
WHEN: Late spring to early summer. Never prune Monterey cypress in the winter. Doing so can kill the tree.

EUCALYPTUS FICIFOLIA

Red-flowering gum

GOAL: Promote a high crown and tall single trunk. Maintain rounded shape.
TYPE: Broadleaf.
HOW TO PRUNE: To train as a tree, gradually remove lowest limbs and begin cutting off side shoots (no more than one-third at a time), starting the second year after planting. Remove suckers as they appear and seed pods after flowering. Little other pruning is needed, although the tree tolerates heavy pruning when overgrown.
WHEN: Spring and summer, after flowering.
TIP: Can be trained as multi-trunked tree.

ILEX

English holly and American holly

GOAL: Maintain the natural pyramidal shape of English (*I. aquifolium*) and American (*I. opaca*) hollies.
TYPE: Broadleaf.
HOW TO PRUNE: Trim wayward growth as needed. To train as a tree, select a single leader when young. Thin vigorous branches to maintain shape. Tolerates shearing.
WHEN: Anytime. Do heavy pruning in early spring, while still dormant.
TIP: Prune berried hollies in December to use the greenery for indoor decorations. Train to one main trunk. Most hollies look best when lower branches remain on tree, but you can limb them up to expose bark. Wear heavy gloves and eye protection.

JUNIPERUS

Junipers

GOAL: Maintain natural form; retain lower branches for trees used as windbreaks.
TYPE: Random buds.
HOW TO PRUNE: Red cedar (*J. virginiana*) requires little pruning. Rocky Mountain juniper (*J. scopulorum*) needs occasional trimming to maintain shape.
WHEN: Major pruning, late winter.
TIP: Red cedar is columnar when young but broadens as it matures.

LAURUS NOBILIS

Bay

GOAL: Control shape and size.
TYPE: Broadleaf.
HOW TO PRUNE: Thin wayward growth as required to maintain shape.
WHEN: Trim in spring or summer. Do heavier pruning before new growth appears.
TIP: Bay is a good candidate for topiary, but if you remove lower branches, be prepared for suckers to develop. Harvest leaves from the prunings to use in cooking.

Bay

English holly

ENCYCLOPEDIA OF EVERGREEN TREES
continued

MAGNOLIA

Southern magnolia and sweet bay magnolia

GOAL: Maintain southern magnolia's (M. *grandiflora*) pyramidal shape and sweet bay's (M. *virginiana*) open habit.
TYPE: Broadleaf.
HOW TO PRUNE: Develop strong central leader when the tree is young. Needs little pruning when mature.
WHEN: Early spring before dormancy is broken.
TIP: Sweet bay magnolia is semievergreen in cold climates. Lower limbs on a southern magnolia catch and hide falling seed pods and browned leaves.

MAYTENUS BOARIA

Mayten

GOAL: Encourage graceful form and maintain semipendulous branching.
TYPE: Broadleaf.
HOW TO PRUNE: Train to single or multiple trunks as desired. Remove suckers and trim branches that droop on ground. Thin crown if it becomes too dense. Remove side growth to develop a tree shape.
WHEN: Spring or fall during the dormant season, before growth begins.

Oriental spruce

OLEA EUROPAEA

Olive tree

GOAL: Encourage a tree form.
TYPE: Broadleaf.
HOW TO PRUNE: Train as a tree by gradually removing lowest branches over four years. Thin lightly as needed to direct growth and allow light to reach interior. For fruiting varieties, remove branches that have fruited. For a multi-trunk tree, select five or fewer strong suckers to train.
WHEN: Anytime for grooming.
TIP: Heavy pruning results in few olives and excessive growth that detracts from the tree's appearance.

PALMS

GOAL: Maintain attractive appearance of the tree and lessen chance of fire hazard.
TYPE: Broadleaf.
HOW TO PRUNE: Remove dead leaves, old flower clusters, and unsightly fronds close to their base. For palms that don't shed old leaf bases, cut off frond. After its base has dried, remove it. Dig out suckers from base of date palm (*Phoenix dactylifera*), Senegal date palm (*P. reclinata*), and others that look best with a single trunk. The trunks of some palms die after flowering. Remove them at ground level.
WHEN: Anytime needed during the year.

Date palm

PICEA

Spruces

GOAL: Maintain pyramidal shape.
TYPE: Terminal buds.
HOW TO PRUNE: Needs little pruning. Increase tree density by cutting new candles in half. If central leader is lost, select and train a new one.
WHEN: Major pruning in winter. Pinch tips in late spring after new growth begins.
TIP: For best appearance or to use the tree as part of a windbreak, leave lower limbs on the tree.

Lacebark pine

PINUS

Pines

GOAL: Depends on species: For some it's to encourage compact, dense growth; for others, to expose exfoliating bark; for all, routine grooming.
TYPE: Terminal buds.
HOW TO PRUNE: Train to a central leader. Pinch off half of each new candle for a fuller tree. Prune dying limbs to trunk. Over three or four years, remove lower limbs of lacebark pine (*P. bungeana*) to expose beautiful bark. Train a replacement if central leader is lost.
WHEN: Spring, after candles elongate but before needles expand.
TIP: Most pine trees are pyramidal when young but develop a flat or rounded top at maturity. Cut only the current season's growth. Eastern white (*P. strobus*) and Scotch pines (*P. sylvestris*) can be sheared as hedges or windbreaks. Monterey pine (*P. radiata*) takes heavy pruning.

PODOCARPUS

Fern pine, maki, and broadleaf or Japanese podocarpus

GOAL: Maintain graceful growth habit and discourage spindly growth.
TYPE: Terminal buds.
HOW TO PRUNE: Requires little beyond shearing to keep in shape. Can train in tree form. Pinch tips of fern pine (*P. gracilior*) or cut it back to ground if overgrown. To maintain weeping habit of broadleaf podocarpus (*P. nagi*), remove competing leaders.
WHEN: Anytime.

PRUNUS

Cherry laurel, Carolina laurel cherry, and Portugal laurel

GOAL: Maintain natural or formal shape.
TYPE: Broadleaf.
HOW TO PRUNE: Natural form: little pruning needed, except to remove dead or damaged wood. Formal shape: shear into hedges or topiaries. Train cherry laurel (*P. caroliniana*) as a tree when young by selecting wide-angled scaffolds and pruning to shape.
WHEN: For formal shapes, after new growth in spring and again in fall; for natural form, in late dormant season. Prune Portugal laurel (*P. lusitanica*) anytime.

PSEUDOTSUGA MENZIESII

Douglas fir

GOAL: Control density and size.
TYPE: Terminal buds.
HOW TO PRUNE: Train to a central leader. Pinch new growth when tree is young. Pinch tips of new side shoots for denser growth and reduced weight on limbs.
WHEN: Before growth begins or in spring after new growth develops to control the size.
TIP: Never top a mature Douglas fir; this causes immediate decline.

PYRUS KAWAKAMII

Evergreen pear

GOAL: Train to a spreading single or multi-trunked tree.
TYPE: Broadleaf.
HOW TO PRUNE:
To train as a tree, remove all but one to three trunks and stake them. Prune lower limbs to desired height. For first five years, shorten branches to outward-facing buds to form a framework.
WHEN: Spring after flowering.
TIP: Evergreen pear is partly deciduous in cold areas. It can be used for espalier or shaped into almost any form.

Prune evergreen pear by training to an outward-facing bud.

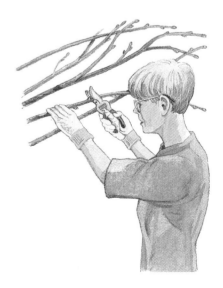

ENCYCLOPEDIA OF EVERGREEN TREES
continued

QUERCUS

Live oak

GOAL: Develop a natural wide-spreading tree with sturdy branches.
TYPE: Broadleaf.
HOW TO PRUNE: Southern live oak (*Q. virginiana*) needs little pruning, only regular grooming. Train California live oak (*Q. agrifolia*) to a central leader while it's young, remove branches below 6 to 12 feet over three to four years. Remove dead and crossing branches. Do not prune unnecessarily.
WHEN: Southern live oak: early winter. California live oak: late winter to early spring while tree is dormant.
TIP: Summer pruning encourages spread of powdery mildew.

SCHINUS MOLLE

Pepper tree

GOAL: Maintain a single leader and protect from storm damage. Shape and keep healthy.
TYPE: Broadleaf.
HOW TO PRUNE: Train when young to a single trunk with branches high enough to walk under. Don't prune branches 4 or more inches in diameter; doing so causes bleeding and fungal diseases. Thin top-heavy growth for a rounded crown. Thin crowded crown to reduce possibility of serious storm damage.
WHEN: Spring, before dormancy breaks, for major cuts. Anytime for touch up.
TIP: Cuts can bleed any time of year.

SCIADOPITYS VERTICILLATA

Umbrella pine or Japanese umbrella pine

GOAL: To create an oriental effect.
TYPE: Terminal buds.
HOW TO PRUNE: Head back upright-growing branches when young to prevent them from becoming multiple leaders. Thin for oriental effect.
WHEN: Anytime.
TIP: Can be used for bonsai. Thin to create the impression of an old tree.

Umbrella pine

Southern live oak

SEQUOIA SEMPERVIRENS

Redwood

GOAL: Encourage a narrow pyramidal form.
TYPE: Random buds.
HOW TO PRUNE: Remove suckers and prune lightly to shape as necessary. Remove lower limbs over three to four years, if desired.
WHEN: Anytime.

SEQUOIADENDRON GIGANTEUM

Giant redwood

GOAL: Maintain pyramidal shape with branches to the ground.
TYPE: Random buds.
HOW TO PRUNE: Little pruning is necessary. Can shear to pyramidal shape when young. Remove dead branches to trunk.
WHEN: Anytime.
TIP: Use as a hedge by planting closely and trimming annually.

TAXUS

Yews

GOAL: Encourage development of a single leader tree with an informal shape.
TYPE: Random buds.
HOW TO PRUNE: To maintain natural form, remove laterals with thinning cuts. For informal hedges, thin about a quarter of the old growth each year.
WHEN: Dormant season for major pruning; anytime to shape and trim.
TIP: Yews can be trained into formal shapes, such as topiaries or hedges. For these shapes, shear twice yearly.

THUJA

Arborvitae and white cedar

GOAL: Encourage natural form or shear into hedge. Regular grooming.
TYPE: Random buds.
HOW TO PRUNE: To shape, occasionally thin, shear, or pinch stem tips. For a hedge form of giant arborvitae (*T. plicata*) with a good top surface, let plants grow 1 foot taller than desired hedge height, then top to 6 inches below desired height. Thin laterals.
WHEN: Late winter for major pruning. Early summer for minor shaping.

TORREYA CALIFORNICA

California nutmeg

GOAL: Maintain shape.
TYPE: Random buds.
HOW TO PRUNE: Needs little except to thin wayward growth. California nutmeg can be cut to the ground if overgrown.
WHEN: Anytime.

TSUGA

Hemlocks

GOAL: Maintain strong central leader, graceful shape, and size.
TYPE: Terminal buds.
HOW TO PRUNE: Train to a central leader and thin to control size and maintain feathery texture. Shear as a formal hedge or windbreak, or thin heavily for informal, natural hedge. Otherwise, little pruning is necessary.
WHEN: Spring or summer.
TIP: If central leader is lost, train nearby branch to take over. Shear in midsummer to encourage dense growth rather than the usual feathery appearance.

UMBELLULARIA CALIFORNICA

California bay, California laurel, Oregon myrtle or pepper wood

GOAL: Maintain attractive appearance.
TYPE: Broadleaf.
HOW TO PRUNE: Needs little pruning except to remove dead material. Shape or thin as needed.
WHEN: Early spring while tree is still dormant.
TIP: In climates that receive snow, train tree to a single trunk. Multiple trunks can crack and admit pathogens that rot the tree.

Oriental thuja

VITEX LUCENS

Chaste tree or New England chaste tree

GOAL: Maintain shape and encourage flowers and fruit.
TYPE: Broadleaf.
HOW TO PRUNE: Requires little pruning beyond cutting out dead or damaged branches. Train when young to a single trunk with well-spaced scaffold branches beginning around 10 feet high.
WHEN: Prune during winter in climates with mild winters; in spring in regions with cold winters.

ENCYCLOPEDIA OF EVERGREEN SHRUBS

Glossy abelia

Unless otherwise noted, these shrubs are broadleaf evergreens.

ABELIA GRANDIFLORA

Glossy abelia

GOAL: Encourage new growth, ample flowers and maintain natural form.
HOW TO PRUNE: Remove winter-killed growth and cut one-third of old stems to the ground each year. If the shrub needs renovating, cut it back to 6 inches tall.
WHEN: Late winter or early spring.
TIP: Blooms on previous season's growth. Also blooms on new growth in warm-winter climates.

ACCA SELLOWIANA

Pineapple guava

GOAL: Train to tree or shrub form.
HOW TO PRUNE: Little pruning is necessary if maintained as a shrub instead of as a tree. Dig out suckers.
WHEN: Late spring.
TIP: Usually grows back from roots if killed by frost.

ARCTOSTAPHYLOS MANZANITA

Manzanita

GOAL: Maintain natural shape.
HOW TO PRUNE: Little needed. To encourage bushiness, pinch back tips.
WHEN: Pinching, spring or early summer. Pruning, late winter.
TIP: Don't cut back to bare growth.

AUCUBA JAPONICA

Aucuba

GOAL: Maintain natural rounded habit and control size.
HOW TO PRUNE: Thin to shorten shrub. Pinch tips of stems to promote bushiness.
WHEN: Late winter or early spring.
TIP: Will tolerate hard pruning to rejuvenate if it becomes leggy. If foliage dies because of canker, prune out dead area; if it dies because of root rot, replace the plants.

AZARA MICROPHYLLA

Boxleaf azara

GOAL: Remove frost-damaged leaves and stems and encourage bushy growth.
HOW TO PRUNE: Clip off faded flower shoots and shorten new growth to promote bushiness. Thin to outside laterals to control height. When allowed to grow in its natural shape, little pruning is needed.
WHEN: Major pruning, early spring. Other work, anytime.
TIP: To rejuvenate, cut one-third of the stems back to the ground each spring for three years.

BERBERIS

Barberries

GOAL: Encourage natural shape and promote new growth.
HOW TO PRUNE: Prune one-fourth of old stems to the ground annually.
WHEN: Late dormant season.
TIP: Because barberries are spiny, wear long sleeves and thorn-proof gloves for protection when pruning.

BUXUS

Boxwoods

GOAL: Maintain desired shape.
HOW TO PRUNE: For a formal planting, shear boxwood. For an informal shape, make thinning cuts using hand pruners.
WHEN: Major pruning in late dormant season. Otherwise, anytime to maintain neatness and shape.
TIP: If damaged or severely overgrown, can cut back to 6 to 12 inches tall.

CALLISTEMON CITRINUS

Bottlebrush

GOAL: Maintain as single-trunked tree, multi-stemmed shrub, or espalier, as desired.
HOW TO PRUNE: Pinch tips to encourage bushiness. Head back a few branches in spring, but don't cut into old growth because bottlebrush doesn't resprout from bare wood.
WHEN: Late dormant season or immediately after flowering.
TIP: Large cuts close very slowly.

CALLUNA

Heather and Scotch heather

GOAL: Keep plant compact.
TYPE: Random buds.
HOW TO PRUNE: Cut back half of previous year's growth. Can also clip back severely.
WHEN: Spring, after flowers fade; early spring if pruning severely.
TIP: Annual pruning keeps heathers looking good for years. Be careful not to cut into old growth.

CAMELLIA

Camellia

GOAL: Maintain shape and stimulate flowering.
HOW TO PRUNE: Train plant when young to encourage single central leader. Remove faded blooms. To encourage bushiness, annually head back to just above the previous year's growth, which will be a lighter color than older growth. Frequent pinching keeps pruning to a minimum. To renovate an overgrown camellia, cut back branches to one-quarter their length. This forces buds to break along the stem. The following spring, thin the top to the desired height.
WHEN: Early spring, after flowering. To shape, anytime. Make major cuts in late dormant season.
TIP: An easy way to shape a camellia is to remove two or three leaves each time you cut off one of the flowers. To encourage larger flowers, but fewer of them, remove flower buds (disbud), leaving only one bud per cluster.

To help shape a camellia, remove two or three leaves with the blossom when cutting for indoor use.

CARPENTERIA CALIFORNICA

Tree anemone

GOAL: Maintain shrub's natural upright shape.
HOW TO PRUNE: Needs little pruning. If the shrub becomes weak or overgrown, cut one-fourth of old stems to the ground annually over a period of four years.
WHEN: After flowering.
TIP: Flowers are produced on the previous season's growth.

CISTUS

Rock rose

GOAL: Encourage bushiness.
HOW TO PRUNE: Keep the plant looking neat by light pruning or tip pinching and removing dead material annually. Heavy pruning isn't desirable or usually needed.
WHEN: After flowering.
TIP: Don't cut back into old growth.

Heather

ENCYCLOPEDIA OF EVERGREEN SHRUBS
continued

CLERODENDRON

Glory flower, lolly bush, pagoda flower, glory bower, and butterfly bush

GOAL: Keep growth in check.
HOW TO PRUNE: Head vigorous growers of this species back hard to control size and shape. Pinch new growth and dig up suckers.
WHEN: Spring.
TIP: Glory flower (*C. bungei*) is deciduous in colder climates. Digging near the roots causes suckering.

CLEYERA JAPONICA

Sakaki

GOAL: Maintain shape.
HOW TO PRUNE: Head back to buds to shape shrub to desired form. Pinch tips of stems to encourage denseness.
WHEN: Pinching in spring. Major pruning, early spring before new growth begins.

Winter daphne

CORREA PULCHELLA

Australian fuchsia or pink Australian fuchsia

GOAL: Encourage branching and abundant flowering.
HOW TO PRUNE: Little pruning necessary. Head back stems to induce branching and greater denseness.
WHEN: Anytime.

COTONEASTER

Cotoneasters

GOAL: Maintain natural shape and encourage formation of berries.
HOW TO PRUNE: Cut branches with sparse growth back to main stem or to ground. Remove dead wood and thin annually. Rejuvenate upright cotoneasters by cutting to 6 inches high.
WHEN: Late winter or early spring.
TIP: Susceptible to fireblight, which causes blackened stems with shepherd's crooks on their ends. When removing diseased area, cut 6 to 12 inches into healthy tissue and disinfect pruners between each cut.

CYTISUS

Broom (also includes *Genista* and *Spartium* species)

GOAL: Control legginess and allow shrub to develop into its natural form while encouraging bushy growth and preventing seed formation, which weakens plants.
HOW TO PRUNE: Pinch new growth back by two-thirds on young shrubs to encourage bushiness. Remove dead stems and spent flowers. Avoid cutting into leafless stem tissue because it won't produce new growth.
WHEN: After flowering.

DAPHNE ODORA

Winter or fragrant daphne

GOAL: Maintain desired shape and promote abundant flowering.
HOW TO PRUNE: Needs little pruning except to remove dieback.
WHEN: After flowering or frequently during bloom period when harvesting cut flowers for bouquets.
TIP: When cutting flowers, make the cuts just above an outward-facing bud if you want a spreading shrub, or clip above an inward-facing bud if you prefer an upright shrub.

DODONAEA VISCOSA

Hopbush

GOAL: Encourage bushiness and control size.
HOW TO PRUNE: Little pruning required except to pinch tips of stems in late spring if growth isn't dense. Thin to restrict size. Can shear into a hedge or train as a single-trunked tree. When the shrub is young, select the most promising stem to be the trunk. Head back shoots that emerge from it as the stem gains strength and remove lower branches.
WHEN: Early spring while dormant.

ELAEAGNUS PUNGENS

Silverberry or thorny elaeagnus

GOAL: Maintain form as desired.
HOW TO PRUNE: Naturally unkempt. Shear or thin into desired shape. Pinch new growth for bushiness. On variegated cultivars, remove stems with leaves that revert to green.
WHEN: After flowering.
TIP: Can prune heavily.

Silverberry

ERICA

Heath

GOAL: To maintain natural form and bountiful blooms.
TYPE: Random buds.
HOW TO PRUNE: Deadhead faded flowers, removing most of previous season's growth, to keep plants compact and free-flowering.
WHEN: Winter- and spring-blooming plants: after flowering and before growth starts. Summer- and fall-blooming heaths: early spring.
TIP: Don't cut into old growth.

ESCALLONIA

Escallonia

GOAL: Maintain upright growth habit and prevent legginess.
HOW TO PRUNE: Thin to shape. Shear, if desired, for a formal hedge. Escallonia is more attractive as a thinned shrub. Cut back to visible buds or to a branch to avoid legginess.
WHEN: Early spring.

EUCALYPTUS ALPINA

Grampian

GOAL: Prevent legginess.
HOW TO PRUNE: Needs little pruning. If growth is rangy, cut stems back to their base.
WHEN: Spring and summer.

EUONYMUS

Winter berry, Japanese euonymus, and spreading euonymus

GOAL: Maintain desired shape and keep growth in bounds.
HOW TO PRUNE: Pinch stem tips to encourage dense growth. Thin older stems occasionally to open up plant and prevent mildew. Remove winter-killed branches.
WHEN: Major pruning in early spring in warm-weather regions. Wait to prune until after last frost in cold-winter regions. Trim in spring and early summer.
TIP: Can prune heavily if necessary.

FATSHEDERA LIZEI

Ivy tree

GOAL: Maintain form.
HOW TO PRUNE: Grow as a shrub and clip frequently, especially to remove errant upright growth. Pinch to encourage bushiness. Cut to ground to rejuvenate.
WHEN: Major pruning, early spring while dormant. Anytime for regular grooming.

Heath

ENCYCLOPEDIA OF EVERGREEN SHRUBS
continued

FATSIA JAPONICA

Japanese fatsia

GOAL: Maintain natural billowy shape.
HOW TO PRUNE: Little pruning needed. Thin any awkward misplaced stems. For best appearance, cut any damaged or unwanted branches back to the trunk.
WHEN: Spring or summer.
TIP: New shoots appear at ground level. Remove those you don't want.

GARDENIA JASMINOIDES

Gardenia

GOAL: Maintain shape and promote abundance of flowers.
HOW TO PRUNE: Little pruning necessary. Pinch tips to encourage branching. Remove faded flower clusters. Thin to reshape as needed. Renovate by cutting back to 6 to 8 inches high.
WHEN: Prune anytime in frost-free areas; spring in colder climates. If winter injury occurs, severely cut back entire shrub. If you remove only the injured branches, the plant will be slow to regrow.
TIP: Blooms on new growth.

Gardenia

GARRYA

Silk tassels

GOAL: Remove wayward growth.
HOW TO PRUNE: Needs little pruning. Can rejuvenate overgrown specimens by cutting one-fourth of stems back to the ground each year for four years.
WHEN: Spring, just after catkins fade and before growth begins.

HEBE

Shrub veronicas

GOAL: Keep shrub compact and encourage blooming.
HOW TO PRUNE: Remove dried stems and winter-damaged growth. Pick off faded flowers and fruit to decrease drain on the plant's energy. Head back stems to encourage bushiness, if needed, and keep plant compact.
WHEN: Spring when dormant. Touch up: all summer, no later than midsummer in areas where the shrub is marginally hardy.
TIP: Tolerates heavy pruning.

Japanese fatsia

HELIANTHEMUM

Rock roses

GOAL: Avoid straggliness and an excessive number of old stems.
HOW TO PRUNE: Pinch new growth when plants are young to encourage a compact shape. Thin as needed.
WHEN: After flowering.

HETEROMELES ARBUTIFOLIA

Christmas berry

GOAL: Promote compact shape.
HOW TO PRUNE: Pinch tips to promote bushiness and thin to control size, if needed. Tolerates heavy pruning if necessary.
WHEN: Late winter or early spring.

HYPERICUM

St. John's worts

GOAL: Control the spread of the plant.
HOW TO PRUNE: On semievergreen aaronsbeard St. John's wort (*H. calycinum*), shear off previous year's growth annually. Prune *H. forrestii* to remove twigs and weak growth. Can prune all stems to the ground to rejuvenate.
WHEN: Early spring for aaronsbeard St. John's wort; spring for *H. forrestii*.

ILEX

Japanese and Chinese holly, inkberry, and box-leaved holly

GOAL: Maintain rounded or pyramidal shape, depending on the species.
HOW TO PRUNE: Minimal pruning is needed, although if a plant threatens to outgrow its space, you can cut it back severely. You can shear all evergreen hollies to a formal shape, if desired. Chinese holly (*I. cornuta*) and Japanese holly (*I. crenata*) can be pruned into formal hedges. Thin inkberry (*I. glabra*).
WHEN: December through early spring.
TIP: Don't cut into old growth.

ILLICIUM

Anise trees

GOAL: Maintain natural shape.
HOW TO PRUNE: Needs little pruning except to control suckers. Purple anise (*I. floridanum*) has compact growth but needs early training.
WHEN: Spring.

JUNIPERUS

Junipers

GOAL: Encourage the plant's natural form and keep growth in check.
TYPE: Random buds.
HOW TO PRUNE: Prune to shape and to limit growth. It's best to start when the plant is young. Thin top branches so they don't shade lower portion of shrub. Keep cuts within the plant, especially on creeping junipers. Remove larger branches of creeping juniper by cutting to a lateral inside the shrub. Keep natural shape in mind. Maintain feathery growth.
WHEN: Spring, when dormant, or early summer preferred, but can prune anytime.
TIP: Junipers can usually be cut back harder than other evergreen shrubs and will regrow from old branches if green leaves are present on the branches. However, don't cut off all the green foliage or the branch won't resprout. If tip blight affects plants in wet weather, disinfect pruners between each cut. Prune stems damaged by rodents.

KALMIA LATIFOLIA

Mountain laurel

GOAL: Maintain health and keep plant in bounds.
HOW TO PRUNE: Remove diseased or dead stems and growth that is out of bounds. Prune lightly, if needed, to keep the plant in shape.
WHEN: After flowering.
TIP: Pinch off dead blooms.

LEPTOSPERMUM LANIGERUM

Teatree

GOAL: Maintain desired shape and compact growth.
HOW TO PRUNE: Requires minimal pruning except to keep center open to light. Cut back to side branches.
WHEN: Early spring.
TIP: Don't prune into a bare branch; no new growth will result.

LEUCOPHYLLUM FRUTESCENS

Texas ranger, Texas sage, or silverleaf

GOAL: Maintain natural form.
HOW TO PRUNE: Thin to desired shape.
WHEN: Winter.
TIP: If growth becomes too rangy, renovate the shrub by cutting it back to 4 inches high.

LEUCOTHOË

Leucothoes

GOAL: Maintain natural arching shape.
HOW TO PRUNE: Not much pruning needed. Prune weak or damaged growth to the ground and cut off spent flowers.
WHEN: After flowering.

To remove a juniper branch, cut to a lateral inside the shrub.

ENCYCLOPEDIA OF EVERGREEN SHRUBS
continued

Japanese mahonia

LIGUSTRUM JAPONICUM

Japanese privet, wax-leaf privet, or privet

GOAL: Maintain shape and check growth.
HOW TO PRUNE: Little pruning needed if grown as an informal shrub. As a formal hedge, shear often to build a strong, wide base. Periodically remove the oldest wood at the ground.
WHEN: Late dormant season for major cutting; anytime for maintaining shape. Shear hedges often throughout summer.
TIP: Makes an excellent screen or hedge.

LOROPETALUM CHINENSE

Chinese witch hazel

GOAL: Encourage a bushy form.
HOW TO PRUNE: Irregularly shaped shrubs need little pruning. Trim lightly or pinch stem tips to encourage bushiness.
WHEN: After spring bloom.
TIP: If you prefer a tree form, prune lower side branches.

MAHONIA

Oregon grapeholly, leatherleaf, Chinese, and Japanese mahonias

GOAL: Maintain attractive, irregular, upright or dense, rounded form, depending on the type of mahonia.
HOW TO PRUNE: Encourage vigorous growth and prevent legginess by cutting one-third of stems to ground each year.
WHEN: After flowering. Before plant breaks dormancy for major pruning; anytime for lighter pruning.

MYOPORUM

GOAL: Remove wayward stems.
HOW TO PRUNE: Doesn't need much pruning except to take off stems growing out of bounds. Cut back severely to rejuvenate. Can prune as a small tree. Remove lower limbs; thin crown annually to decrease wind damage.
WHEN: Late winter, while dormant, or anytime.

MYRICA

Wax myrtle, bayberry, or candleberry

GOAL: Maintain desired shape.
HOW TO PRUNE: Needs little pruning except to remove winter-damaged branches. If desired, you can shear wax myrtle as a hedge or train it into a small tree.
WHEN: Spring.
TIP: Some species are deciduous.

MYRTUS COMMUNIS

Myrtle

GOAL: Maintain desired shape.
HOW TO PRUNE: Little pruning is needed to maintain myrtle as an informal shrub. Shear it as a formal hedge or topiary, or remove lower limbs to train it into a small tree. To decrease height, thin the tallest stems.
WHEN: Anytime.

NANDINA DOMESTICA

Heavenly bamboo

GOAL: Encourage new growth and preserve interesting upright habit. Prevent legginess.
HOW TO PRUNE: Dwarfs need little pruning. Remove winter damage and thin out-of-bounds growth. For tall, upright-growing nandinas in areas with mild or moderate winters, cut four of the oldest canes to the ground yearly. Pinch tips to maintain constant height.
WHEN: Pruning: late winter or early spring. Pinching: late spring.
TIP: Plant dies back to ground when temperature reaches 0° F. It will resprout from the roots. Tolerates severe pruning.

Heavenly bamboo

NERIUM OLEANDER

Oleander

GOAL: Limit size and promote bushiness.
HOW TO PRUNE: Shorten stems that have grown too long. Cut one-fourth of the oldest stems to the ground. Pinch tips to encourage bushiness. Cut shrub to ground to renovate.
WHEN: Just before new growth starts.

OSMANTHUS FRAGRANS

Fragrant olive, tea olive, or sweet olive

GOAL: Maintain desired shape.
HOW TO PRUNE: Little required but can be sheared into a hedge.
WHEN: Anytime.

PAXISTIMA CANBYI

Cliff green, rat stripper, or canby paxistima

GOAL: Maintain low-growing, spreading shape.
HOW TO PRUNE: Rarely needed. Can pinch back if needed.
WHEN: Spring.

PHOTINIA

Photinias

GOAL: Limit size and promote new growth.
HOW TO PRUNE: Shearing lightly in late spring and in summer results in more red foliage. Thin to maintain size and shape. Cut to ground to renovate. When young, train to multiple stems, selecting the most vigorous. Can be pruned as a small tree or standard. Prune fraser photinia (P. × fraseri) when young to encourage basal branching and Chinese photinia (P. serrulata) to control size.
WHEN: Spring through midsummer. Avoid pruning late in summer in northern limit of hardiness.

PIERIS JAPONICA

Japanese pieris, lily-of-the-valley bush, or andromeda

GOAL: Shape shrub as needed and encourage blossoming.
HOW TO PRUNE: Remove faded flowers and other dead material. Thin leggy growth.
WHEN: After flowering.
TIP: Don't let seed pods ripen. If you cut back into a bare stem, only one shoot will sprout; several stems will sprout if you cut into a group of leaves. Blooms on old wood.

PINUS MUGO

Mugo pine

GOAL: Maintain desired form and keep plant in bounds.
TYPE: Terminal buds.
HOW TO PRUNE: Pinch off half of each new candle each year.
WHEN: In spring, after candles elongate but before they expand.

PITTOSPORUM

Japanese or tobira pittosporum

GOAL: Maintain desired form and size.
HOW TO PRUNE: Shear for formal hedge or thin errant stems for a shrub with a natural shape. To renovate, prune heavily.
WHEN: Anytime.
TIP: You can train pittosporum as a tree, but growing it as a shrub is most common.

Photinia

ENCYCLOPEDIA OF EVERGREEN SHRUBS
continued

PRUNUS

English or cherry laurel

GOAL: Control size and shape.
HOW TO PRUNE: Thin as needed to maintain shape. Trim frequently in warm climates.
WHEN: Anytime.

PYRACANTHA

Pyracantha or firethorn

GOAL: Control wayward growth. Becomes wild and wooly when unpruned.
HOW TO PRUNE: Thin dense growth so light reaches interior of plant. Remove suckers. If growing as espalier, remove excess growth throughout the growing season.
WHEN: After flowering.
TIP: Wear thorn-proof gloves when pruning. Shearing reduces number of berries.

RAPHIOLEPIS INDICA

Indian hawthorn

GOAL: Promote bushiness.
HOW TO PRUNE: Little pruning necessary. Pinch tips to cause more dense growth.
WHEN: Spring and summer.
TIP: If plant is grafted, remove suckers that appear.

RHODODENRONS AND AZALEAS

GOAL: Shape, control size, and encourage branching.
HOW TO PRUNE: Remove spent blooms. Thin to a branch or dormant bud to shape, control size, and maintain horizontal branching. For more compact azaleas and better blooms the following year, pinch faded flowers and tips of stems. To prune rhododendrons, remove the large growth bud at the top of each rosette of leaves, then pinch shoots just after they have started growing but before they expand. May rejuvenate rhododendron by cutting one-fifth to one-third of stems to ground each year for three to five years.
PRUNE: Immediately after flowering or in late dormant season.
TIP: Shearing azaleas during summer removes the flower buds, which form at this time, and results in an unnatural-looking plant.

Pyracantha

SARCOCOCCA

Sweet box

GOAL: Encourage vigor and keep growth in check.
HOW TO PRUNE: When shrub becomes crowded, cut one-third of oldest stems to ground each year for three years. With species that spread by underground runners, remove unwanted stems. You can also renovate sweet box by completely cutting the stems back to their base.
WHEN: Anytime.

Sweet box

SKIMMIA

Skimmias

GOAL: Maintain the natural form.
TYPE: Broadleaf.
HOW TO PRUNE: Needs minimal pruning. Remove dead branches and shape as necessary.
WHEN: Summer.

TAXUS

Yews

GOAL: Maintain natural shape.
TYPE: Random buds.
HOW TO PRUNE: Use heading and thinning cuts to direct size and shape. Cutting tips of stems results in a denser plant. Shear as required for a hedge. Rejuvenate by heading to 6 to 12 inches tall. For informal hedges, thin about a quarter of the old growth each year.
WHEN: Shearing, early spring and during growing season. Pruning, late winter or early spring.
TIP: Yews will sometimes regrow even when cut back hard to bare wood.

VIBURNUM

Leatherleaf, mapleleaf, hobblebush, and service viburnums

GOAL: Maintain natural shape.
HOW TO PRUNE: Evergreen viburnums need little pruning. You may want to occasionally shorten and thin branches. Leatherleaf viburnum (*V. rhytidophyllum*) becomes open with age. Prune it to the ground to rejuvenate.
WHEN: In early spring for major pruning. After blooming for minor trimming.

XYLOSMA CONGESTUM

Shiny xylosma

GOAL: To maintain naturally rounded shape or other desired form.
HOW TO PRUNE: If grown as an informal, naturally rounded shrub, shiny xylosma needs almost no pruning. Can be sheared into a tree shape, topiary, or hedge.
WHEN: After blooming to shape; while still dormant, for major pruning.
TIP: May be deciduous in colder areas. Train as an espalier or as a single or multi-trunked tree. Remove lower branches.

YUCCA

Adam's needle, soapweed, or Spanish dagger

GOAL: Maintain natural shape.
HOW TO PRUNE: Remove flower stalks at base. Cut off dead leaves.
WHEN: After flowering.
TIP: Watch out for the sharply pointed leaves on this shrub.

Yew

Shiny xylosma

PRUNING FRUITING TREES, SHRUBS, AND VINES

One of the joys of gardening is harvesting ripe apples, blueberries, or raspberries from your own yard. But that doesn't happen without lots of pruning, beginning when the plant is small and continuing each year afterward.

Early pruning is needed to establish a strong framework of branches that won't break under the weight of a large crop of fruit. Once that's achieved, you must prune each year to increase the amount of sunlight reaching the plant's interior to ensure a good harvest, to limit plant size, and to remove unproductive branches for easier access to the fruit at harvest time and when spraying the plant. An open habit also increases air circulation and cuts down on fungal diseases, which can be a problem with some types of fruit.

Sunshine is vital to the growth and ripening of every kind of fruit, so all pruning and training methods are geared to maximize the amount of light the plant receives. Shaded fruit will be small and of poor quality.

Also important is the angle of the branches. When scaffold branches form a narrow angle with the trunk, they're weakly attached and likely to break off. In addition, narrow crotches produce vigorous tip growth but few flowers and fruit. Conversely, a crotch that's too wide—with an angle greater than 60 degrees—tends to grow water sprouts which don't produce fruit.

To train a young branch to form a 45- to 60-degree angle, attach a spreader between the trunk and the stem, as shown in the illustration at left. Spreaders are available at garden centers and in mail-order catalogs, but clothespins work just as well. You also can tie weights to branches or tie branches to other branches. Leave spreaders in place until the branch stays at the desired angle on its own. If water sprouts appear on the branch, you've spread it too wide. Prune the water sprouts and decrease the angle.

Use a scrap of wood to spread branches to a 60-degree angle. At wider angles, water sprouts form at the expense of fruit.

PRUNING FRUIT TREES

The goal when pruning fruit trees is to produce as much high-quality fruit as possible. The tree's branches must be strong and shouldn't shade each other. To achieve that objective, there are three main forms for pruning fruit trees: central leader, modified

CENTRAL LEADER TRAINING

YEAR 1

Choose the scaffolds and head them and the leader back by a quarter to a half to promote branching.

YEAR 2

In late winter of the next year, again head back the leader as well as the new scaffolds.

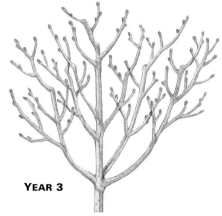

YEAR 3

In the third year, develop the last tier of scaffolds. From then on, prune as usual to keep the tree healthy.

central leader, and vase (sometimes called open center). The technique you use depends on the fruit species.

CENTRAL LEADER:

Fruit trees trained to a central leader have a single upright trunk and two or three tiers of well-spaced scaffold branches. Use this system for apples and pears.

After planting a "whip" (young, unbranched tree) in spring, cut it back to a bud 18 to 24 inches above the ground for a dwarf tree, 28 to 36 inches for a full-size tree. This causes the whip to branch.

In early summer, select one of the new upright limbs to be the leader; remove all other upright branches. If necessary, use spreaders to develop correct crotch angles.

After the tree goes dormant, choose two to three branches to be scaffolds. These should be evenly spaced around the tree, pointing in different directions, and 6 to 8 inches apart vertically. Prune off all other limbs. In late winter, trim the central leader to 24 to 30 inches above the uppermost scaffold to promote growth of the second tier of scaffolds. At the same time, cut back the first-year scaffolds by one-third to one-half (to an outward-facing bud) to encourage secondary branching. Also remove any shoots competing with the central leader.

In the second summer, insert more spreaders if needed and select the limbs to be the second tier of scaffolds. Remove branches between the two tiers, shoots on the trunk, and suckers at the tree base. Then, in late winter, head back the new scaffolds and the leader, and thin branches competing with the scaffolds.

The third summer, select the last tier of scaffolds. Watch for water sprouts or suckers, and use spreaders to ensure wide crotch angles. For standard fruit trees, you may continue this same method for several more years, but dwarfs will have reached their optimal height. Let the central leader continue to grow.

MODIFIED CENTRAL LEADER:

Both sweet and sour cherry trees are pruned in a modified central-leader style, and apples are occasionally trained in this way. This system is a combination of central leader and vase training, which results in a strong tree with a center open to sunlight.

Apples produce best when trained to a central leader or modified central leader structure.

For the first three years after planting, train the tree to a central leader. When the tree has six to eight scaffolds and is 6 feet tall, cut the leader back to the top scaffold branch in late winter. Also, head the scaffolds. From then on, follow vase-training methods.

VASE TRAINING:

With vase training, also called open-center training, the tree is shaped to have a short trunk with three to four wide-spreading scaffolds. This form allows light to penetrate to all the branches. Vase training is especially useful for peaches, nectarines, apricots, and plums. Cherries are sometimes trained in this way also.

After planting, cut the whip to a bud 24 inches high for dwarf trees or 30 inches for standard-size trees. Trim any branches below the cut to three buds.

For a modified central leader, train as a central-leader tree the first three years. When tree is 6 feet tall, cut the leader to the top scaffold and head back remaining scaffolds.

PRUNING FRUIT TREES
continued

VASE TRAINING

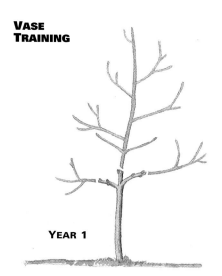

YEAR 1

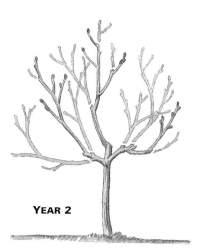

YEAR 2

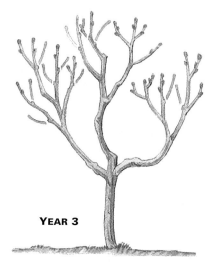

YEAR 3

Cut the young, dormant tree back to 2 feet. Prune branches remaining below the cut to three buds.

Remove all but the branches you selected for the scaffolds and head them back to outward-facing buds.

Continue thinning the tree to keep its center open to sunlight. Head branches to outward-facing buds.

In midsummer after planting, select the three or four best branches to be scaffolds. These should radiate evenly around the trunk and be spaced equally apart. Tip back these branches to reduce apical dominance and encourage wider crotches. Late the next winter, remove all growth except the scaffolds. However, if the tree has fewer than three good scaffolds, let a vertical stem continue to grow to produce more. Head the selected scaffolds to outward-facing buds.

After developing the scaffold structure, pruning can focus on removing any growth that closes the center of the tree, such as water sprouts and crossing branches.

THINNING FRUIT

One of the best things you can do for fruit trees is to thin the excess fruit. After waiting three years to pick the first apple, it's hard to believe there could be "excess" fruit. But the benefits of thinning are numerous.

Thinning increases both the size and the quality of fruit, prevents limbs from breaking under a heavy load, and avoids alternate-year bearing in which a small crop follows an especially large one.

Large fruits, such as apples, mature best when spaced 6 inches apart on the stem. Space peaches and nectarines 4 to 6 inches and apricots 2 to 3 inches from each other. The best time to remove the young fruit is when it reaches about ½ inch in diameter. Waiting to thin the crop until midsummer will adversely affect the next year's crop.

TIPS FOR TREE FRUITS

APPLES: Apples are usually trained to either a central or modified central leader. Fruit grows in clusters on short spurs. After the "June drop" of immature fruit (which occurs earlier than June in warm climates), thin them to one apple per cluster about 6 inches apart. Don't injure the flower spur when you prune; leave the apple stem attached to the tree.

APRICOTS: Apricots are trained to a modified central leader. Take care to ensure wide branch angles. Each year after the tree flowers, prune lightly to encourage growth of new spurs on which the fruit grows. Remove spurs that are no longer productive.

CHERRIES: Most cherries are grown by the modified central leader style. Because sour cherries bear fruit on young spurs or branch tips, prune out wood that's more than three to five years old. On both sweet and sour cherries, remove spurs that do not bear fruit, as well as unfruitful branches. If there's a chance of a late frost, delay pruning until after flowering to avoid damage. Otherwise, prune in early spring.

CITRUS: Citrus often needs little pruning except to remove dead or weak branches and to thin twiggy growth. Lemons usually require the most pruning, especially to remove suckers and to head branches for a compact habit. Cut back long branches at the tips to promote shoots nearer the center of the tree.

FIGS: Figs bear on wood that is a year old and often produce a second crop on the current season's growth. In cold climates, figs are usually grown in a shrub shape; in warmer regions, they're often grown as a tree. Don't head back the shrubby forms. Remove winter damage and branches that are touching the ground. Train fig trees into a vase shape.

PEACHES AND NECTARINES: Train peaches and nectarines to a vase or open-center tree. Fruit forms on the previous year's growth. In areas where winter damage is possible, wait until early spring to prune because wounds will close faster as growth begins. Waiting also gives you a chance to see how many flower buds survived the cold. Use thinning cuts to keep the center of the tree open. Thin fruit to 4 to 6 inches apart.

PEARS: Train pears to a central leader and lightly prune them annually to remove water sprouts or limbs that rub against one another. Hand-thin fruit to 5 inches apart. If leaves suddenly turn brown, look scalded, and the tip of the stem develops a shepherd's crook, the tree has fireblight, a bacterial disease that's especially troublesome on pears. Immediately prune back affected stems 12 inches into healthy tissue, taking care to disinfect your pruners between each cut to avoid spreading the disease.

PERSIMMONS: Train persimmons to a modified central leader and shorten long, willowy shoots when young. Hand thin oriental persimmon fruit so that remaining fruit grows larger. (American persimmons will remain small whether you thin them or not.)

PLUMS: Train European plums to a central leader and Japanese plums to a vase form. Plums fruit on year-old wood and on spurs on older branches. Because the fruiting spurs of Japanese plums are only about 3 inches long, compared to the 3-foot spurs of European plums, they need much more thinning to be productive. Also, Japanese plum spurs bear for six to eight years. Hand thin plums to 2 to 3 inches apart.

RENOVATING TREES

If you inherit a fruit tree that hasn't been properly cared for and is unproductive, first assess its problems. Look for diseases, insects, little or no light reaching the interior, growth that's too dense or tall, or poor fruit set. Then you'll know where to make corrections.

REJUVENATING AN OVERGROWN APPLE TREE

First, remove dead, damaged branches, limbs that cross or grow downward, and water sprouts. Shorten upright branches by cutting back to an outward-growing limb of the same diameter. Take three or four years to rejuvenate severely overgrown trees.

Renovating a fruit tree is a three-year project, and the tree probably won't bear a full crop for at least two years after that. However, many gardeners enjoy making an unfruitful tree productive again.

The time to start renovating a fruit tree is in late winter. The first year, remove dead, injured, diseased and crossing branches, suckers, and branches growing downward. Reduce the height of the crown as well as thin it to let in sunlight. Thin crowded apple and pear spurs. As always, take care to never remove more than one-fourth of the tree at one time.

Repeat the procedure the next winter, also pruning water sprouts and odd clusters of new shoots that may have developed over the growing season. Remove weak branches and crowded growth. The third winter, continue thinning as needed.

Thinning the fruit set actually results in larger fruit of higher quality. As a guide, space apples and pears at 6 inches, peaches and nectarines at 4 to 6 inches and apricots and

PRUNING NUT TREES

Nut trees—except for filberts or hazelnuts—grow into extremely large trees. They are beautiful when grown to maturity but are not suitable for small yards. Most are subject to disease and insects.

ALMONDS: These trees bear fruit on 1-year-old shoots. The ultimate goal for an almond tree is to train it to into a wide tree with an open top. Prune back upward-growing branches to laterals that grow outward. This creates a wider branching habit.

CHESTNUTS: The chestnut trees that are generally available for home planting include European chestnut, Chinese chestnut, and hybrids. The American chestnut can only be grown safely in blight-free regions west of the Rockies.

Chestnut trees grow rapidly, starting to bear in about three to five years after planting. They bear on new wood. Pruning is not necessary for a good fruit set. Train young trees to a central leader. Once that framework is established, trees need only occasional pruning to remove dead, weak, or poorly placed branches.

FILBERTS (HAZELNUTS): The standard nut-producing filberts often grow into huge, suckering shrubs that form thickets in time. They are usually trained into small trees, reaching 15 to 25 feet tall. Filberts form on year-old wood, so as plantings age, remove older, unproductive stems. Head back remaining branches to encourage new growth (as you would for peaches, only not as heavily). Filbert nuts are small, and a large bearing surface is necessary for a good crop. The trees usually start to bear fruit at four years.

PECANS: Little pruning is needed for pecan trees other than lateral pruning to limit tree size. Pecans bear on new wood. Train them to a central leader framework, heading back any overly vigorous laterals that would divert energy from upward growth. Trees start to bear in five to eight years.

WALNUTS: Like pecans, walnuts bear on new wood and need a minimum of annual pruning after the initial shape is established. Some heavy-bearing varieties require pruning to thin them.

PRUNING BRAMBLES

1

2

3

Last year's growth is blooming and bearing fruit as new shoots emerge. Remove all but five of the new shoots (1). After harvest, cut all bearing canes to the ground. Tie the five new canes to the wire (2). Head them back a few inches to promote lateral growth along the wire (3). After harvesting from these new canes in fall, head them back (4). In winter, cut these lateral branches back to 18 inches long. They will bear the coming summer, continuing the cycle (5).

4

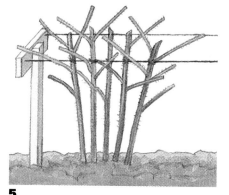

5

PRUNING SHRUBBY FRUIT

Fruit that grows on shrubs are much easier to care for than tree fruit because they need much less pruning. Some, such as blueberries, require only enough pruning to stimulate production of large, juicy berries, but others need more attention.

BRAMBLES

BOYSENBERRIES, BLACKBERRIES, AND LOGANBERRIES all have biennial canes. The canes emerge from the crown and grow a year before bearing. After bearing, the cane becomes barren or dies. For that reason, they need annual pruning.

Start at planting time. Cut all the canes to ground level. As the new canes grow, train them to a trellis with one wire 3 feet high and another 5 feet high. A single wire is fine for erect or non-trailing forms of these fruit.

In following years, prune erect brambles twice annually, in summer and again in late winter. In summer after harvest, remove the spent canes; tie new canes to the trellis and pinch their tips. These new canes will bear fruit in late summer. After harvest, cut back the portion that fruited. Then in late winter trim the lateral branches to 18 inches. These will be the first to bear fruit the next summer.

Prune trailing blackberries in late winter by first cutting down the spent canes. Thin the remaining canes, leaving six to nine per plant. Shorten long canes to about 7 feet. Trim the side branches to 18 inches long.

RASPBERRIES bear fruit either once in summer—summer-bearing or single crop—or twice in summer and fall—everbearing.

Cut spent fruiting stems of summer-bearing types right after harvest. Tie the new canes to the trellis, thinning out the weakest ones. In late winter, thin the canes so that they're 6 to 10 inches apart at the base.

Everbearing raspberries fruit twice (once in summer and again in fall) before the cane dies. Prune them only after the second crop, as with boysenberries and loganberries.

CURRANTS

RED AND WHITE CURRANTS fruit on two- and three-year-old stems and also at the base of year-old shoots. In spring at planting, cut all but three of the strongest stems to ground level. The next year, leave those stems along with three of the best canes that grew after planting. Remove all other canes. Aim for an even blend of one-, two-, and three-year-old stems, so in the fourth winter, cut all four-year-old stems to the ground.

BLACK CURRANTS bear on one- and two-year-old growth, so they should be pruned to promote new stem growth each year. Remove all but three stems at planting and cut those back to one bud apiece. In early spring of the next year, cut out weak stems. The following dormant season, cut all stems more than two years old to the ground, leaving 10 shoots.

ELDERBERRIES

Elderberries spread by suckers. You'll have to thin them, cutting to ground level. Remove stems more than three years old. The shrubs fruit on the previous year's growth.

GOOSEBERRIES

Gooseberries bear on year-old wood and on spurs on older wood. When planting, cut back all but six stems to the ground. From then on, remove the three-year-old stems. Thin the shrub to an open form.

BLUEBERRIES

Before the fourth year, no pruning is needed except to remove dead or diseased material. However, remove flowers the first year after planting to boost root growth. In subsequent years, remove three-year-old or older stems in winter to open the interior and reduce plant size. Adjust the number of canes you take off each year by the size of the berries. If berries are small, prune more heavily that winter. If they have been large, you can do less pruning.

Blueberries, gooseberries, and other shrubby fruit need occasional thinning. Thinning lets light into the interior, which helps increase fruit size. Blueberries fruit on one-year-old wood. Remove oldest branches with twiggy growth rather than strong year-old growth. Gooseberries fruit on one- and two-year-old wood, so remove branches older than that.

PRUNING VINES

From grapes to kiwis, vining fruits are some of the most popular grown. Here's how they're pruned.

There are two popular pruning methods for grapes: spur and cane. Although there are exceptions, spur pruning is recommended

PRUNING GRAPES

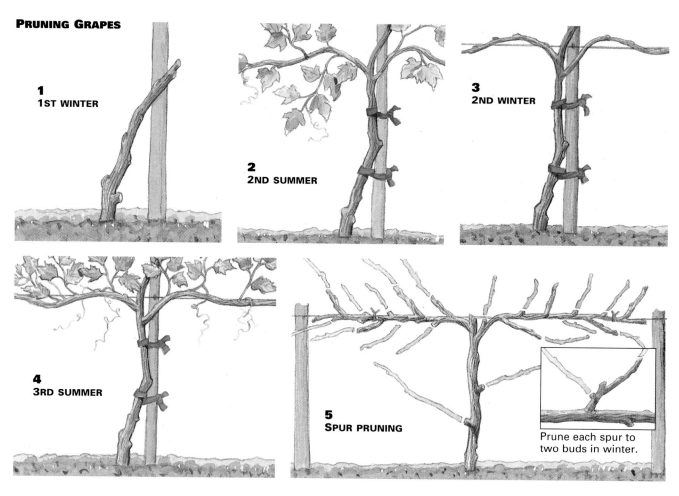

1 1ST WINTER

2 2ND SUMMER

3 2ND WINTER

4 3RD SUMMER

5 SPUR PRUNING

Prune each spur to two buds in winter.

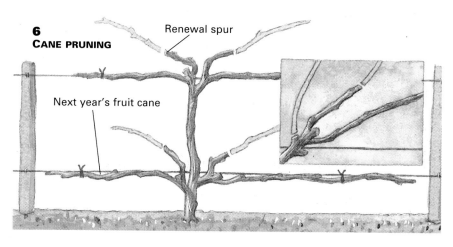

6 CANE PRUNING

Renewal spur

Next year's fruit cane

During the first winter after planting, cut all but the strongest shoot back to the ground. Head the remaining shoot to four buds (1). The next summer, when new shoots grow to 12 inches long, select the most vigorous and pinch all the others off at the trunk. Tie the remaining shoot to the trellis. Let it grow to the top of the wire, then pinch it (2). The next winter cut off all but the main trunk and two strong side branches (3). Again, let the vine grow through the summer, but pinch sprouts that develop on the trunk (4). For spur pruning, remove the weakest side branches in winter and trim the ones remaining to two buds (5). In cane pruning, clip the four strongest laterals to 10 buds long and tie them to the trellis. Trim four other strong shoots to two buds to be renewal spurs for the next year (6).

for European varieties and muscadines, while cane pruning is reserved for American varieties and French-American hybrids, as well as 'Thompson Seedless'. Your local extension service office will be able to help if you're not sure what type of grape you have.

THE FIRST THREE YEARS

FIRST YEAR: For the four-arm Kniffen system, set up a sturdy trellis with the posts about 6 feet tall and 15 to 20 feet apart. Stretch strong galvanized wire between the posts at 2½ and 5 feet high.

Plant the young vine next to a post at the same depth it grew in the nursery and cut it back to two buds. During its first summer, let the vine grow naturally. The first winter after planting, remove all shoots except for the strongest. Head it back to three or four buds.
SECOND YEAR: The next summer, new shoots will break from those buds. After they reach a foot long, select the most vigorous one to be the trunk and tie it to the support. Remove the others.

When the trunk grows as tall as the bottom wire, pinch or head it back to force branching. Tie two of the resulting new shoots to the wire, and let a third one grow up to the next wire. Pinch it when it reaches the top wire.

In winter, prune each horizontal branch to 10 buds and tip back the trunk.
THIRD YEAR: The third summer after planting, let the vine grow, pinching off shoots that sprout from the trunk. After this, train the vine to either a spur or cane system.

SPUR PRUNING

Because the first few buds of European and muscadine grapes are the most fruitful, prune these grapes hard each winter. Remove the weakest shoots growing from the horizontal "arms" along with any shoots on the trunk. Cut the shoots remaining—the spurs—to two buds. Space the spurs 6 to 10 inches apart.

Each spur will produce two shoots that will fruit the next summer. In the winter after they fruit, cut them back to two buds. Also, remove any weak growth and clear new growth from the main trunk.

CANE PRUNING

Because the fruitful shoots of American and French-American varieties are produced farther along the branches than those of European varieties and muscadines, they are pruned to canes. This system leaves longer branches than those of spur-pruned types, but fewer of them.

In the third winter after planting, trim off all but eight horizontal branches. Four will be fruiting canes the next year. Trim them to 10 buds each and tie them to the trellis. Prune the other four lateral shoots to two buds. These will become renewal spurs, which will bear fruit the following year.

Every winter thereafter, cut off the cane that fruited. Select the two strongest shoots that grew from the renewal spurs. Cut one to 10 buds and tie to the wire. Cut the next strongest shoot to two or three buds. Remove the weakest shoots along with any shoots that developed on the trunk.

KIWIS

When growing kiwis for fruit, train the vine to a 6-foot-high trellis with three to five wires strung between T-shaped supports (see illustration below).

Like grapes, kiwis bear fruit on year-old wood. So much of their training is similar to that of a cane-pruned grape. Limit the vine to one main stem the first year as you train it to the trellis. When the vine reaches the wires, pinch its tip to force branching. Train two of the resulting shoots (the arms) in each direction along the wires and remove all other shoots.

Each winter, pinch the shoots to develop lateral branches about 2 feet apart. Fruit will grow on the resulting branches.

After plants become established, cut the arms back to 7 feet each year in early spring and shorten the laterals to eight buds. Laterals will produce fruit for three years, after which you should remove them, cutting them back to a bud on the main trunk.

Prune hardy kiwis like grapes. Develop a strong framework, then train to keep a constant supply of year-old fruiting side branches.

INDEX

Page numbers in Italics denote information in photographs only. Numbers in boldface refer to encyclopedia entries.

METRIC CONVERSIONS

U.S. Units to Metric Equivalents			Metric Units to U.S. Equivalents		
To Convert From	Multiply By	To Get	To Convert From	Multiply By	To Get
Inches	25.4	Millimeters	Millimeters	0.0394	Inches
Inches	2.54	Centimeters	Centimeters	0.3937	Inches
Feet	30.48	Centimeters	Centimeters	0.0328	Feet
Feet	0.3048	Meters	Meters	3.2808	Feet
Yards	0.9144	Meters	Meters	1.0936	Yards
Square inches	6.4516	Square centimeters	Square centimeters	0.1550	Square inches
Square feet	0.0929	Square meters	Square meters	10.764	Square feet
Square yards	0.8361	Square meters	Square meters	1.1960	Square yards
Acres	0.4047	Hectares	Hectares	2.4711	Acres
Cubic inches	16.387	Cubic centimeters	Cubic centimeters	0.0610	Cubic inches
Cubic feet	0.0283	Cubic meters	Cubic meters	35.315	Cubic feet
Cubic feet	28.316	Liters	Liters	0.0353	Cubic feet
Cubic yards	0.7646	Cubic meters	Cubic meters	1.308	Cubic yards
Cubic yards	764.55	Liters	Liters	0.0013	Cubic yards

To convert from degrees Fahrenheit (F) to degrees Celsius (C), first subtract 32, then multiply by ⁵⁄₉.

To convert from degrees Celsius to degrees Fahrenheit, multiply by ⁹⁄₅, then add 32.